D1588187

The GREATEST
in the WORLD

Lindsay Henson

The Greatest
Tax Tips
in the World

A 'The Greatest in the World' book

www.thegreatestintheworld.com

Cover images:
© Maria P; © Julien Tromeur
both courtesy of www.foltolia.com, © Chris Lynn

Layout:
Shazia Saleemi
www.designspirit.co.uk

Copy editor:
Bronwyn Robertson
www.theartsva.com

Series creator/editor:
Steve Brookes

Published in 2008 by
The Greatest in the World Ltd, PO Box 3182,
Stratford-upon-Avon, Warwickshire CV37 7XW

Text and design Copyright © 2008 – The Greatest in the World Ltd

A CIP catalogue record for this book is available from the British Library
ISBN 978-1-905151-43-1

Printed and bound in Italy by Printer Trento s.r.l.

This book is dedicated to all my clients who have suffered (not always in silence) the stresses and strains of a full-blown investigation by HM Revenue and Customs. They've been grilled and bullied (and that's just at my hands!) to enable me to fight their corner. I've loved every minute of it and made many good friends in the process.

Without the constant support of my wonderfully patient and always humorous husband Martyn, who has acted as cook, cleaner and chauffeur to our daughter Madeleine, I would never have had the luxury of time to write this. Perhaps now I shall return to my household duties – or perhaps not!

Special thanks to my "Work Wise Women" networking group partner and true friend Sarah Brattan, who's unconditional support and enthusiasm kept me believing that tax really isn't boring!

Grateful thanks to Fiona McVeigh of FLM Secretarial Services, Carolyn Sutherland and Sue Mason for helping this I.T. imbecile with the typing and editing and last, but not at all least, apologies to my kids Sophie and Maddie and mum Dorothy, for listening to the constant ramblings of a tax geek.

Contents

A few words from Lindsay…

Working as an Inland Revenue Tax Inspector in sunny Torquay back in 1992, I took the somewhat risky decision to turn my back on the cosy 'job for life' and index-linked pension, and move out of my comfort zone to become the proverbial 'gamekeeper turned poacher'.

Yes, the full backing of the Taxes Acts may well have wielded a certain power, but in the popularity stakes, I was definitely bottom of the Hit Parade – now that certainly dates me!

On the basis that 'everyone deserves a defence' and armed with invaluable inside knowledge, I signed up with a firm of chartered accountants to offer my services in representing those who fall foul of the Taxman. There's never been any shortage of work as sadly 'tax' is a club we all have a lifetime membership of – potentially from the cradle to the grave and sometimes even beyond! It is those who fail to join the club (or let their subscription lapse!) who come my way, to take what can be a long and scary journey. I often say, the taxman doesn't suffer from stress, but he's a carrier!

Using my experience from 'the other side' I have developed my hands-on approach to keep the taxman's hands off your money. Life is never dull and invariably there's a humorous side – often at the Revenue's expense.

At the end of my career, I hope that those on both sides of the taxman's desk would say that I was approachable and fair and always went that extra mile.

As a frustrated actor I have also taken great pleasure in guest lecturing on cruise ships, as well as speaking to fellow professionals. 'Talking Tax' is what I do and to be asked to spread the word as part of this tremendous series of books is indeed a pleasure and a thrill.

I trust you'll find the Tax Tips clear, practical, rewarding and dare I say it – entertaining; not a word normally found in the same sentence as TAX! It's not a textbook, nor is it too technical or exhaustive. There are many of those written for, and by, the experts. As tax is an annual moveable feast with laws changing literally as I write, the book has a reasonable shelf-life to make it great value for you, Joe and Joanne Public, who come my way every day.

Tax isn't rocket science, nor is it always an exact science, and if I am able to save you at least the price of this little book then it's a job well done – after all, you must have been curious to have picked it up!

Many happy returns!

Lindsay x

PS: I apologise in advance for my terminology as I often refer to HM Revenue and Customs (HMRC) as the Revenue or the Taxman when there are just as likely to be an equal number of Taxwomen as men!

Client Testimonials

For Lindsay with many thanks & laughs!

During a period of difficulties, Lindsay steered us (at 60 mph!) from confusion and despair towards positive thinking and a resolution. She was, and remains, professional, positive and pragmatic. When the chips were down for us Lindsay poured oil (vegetable oil, of course) onto our troubled waters.

Rick and Jenny Welbourn
DJ's Fish Shop

Lindsay Henson's talents with tax are second to none. She is fast, fearless and phenomenally clever – a formidable ally. They don't come any better than Lindsay and now with this book everyone can have the benefit of her invaluable advice.

Julie Peasgood
Actress and TV Presenter

Lindsay Henson is always on hand to provide excellent, reliable and up to date advice. She has an unerring ability to produce prompt solutions to your tax problems. She has an encyclopaedic knowledge of current tax legislation together with the flexibility to think on her feet. When in doubt I always consult her.

Kevin Fitzpatrick
Accountant, London

The brown envelope sat there menacingly, I opened it and my stomach sank. Even though I knew I was straight with HMRC, I am not the best organised person in the world and the thought of going over the last six years filled me with dread. My feelings didn't change over the next six weeks; in fact they got worse, with my then-accountants going back and forth in their suits, the Revenue asking for more and more details and me digging deeper and deeper in old boxes. Expecting a knock at the door any day from the Inspector with his surgical rubber gloves on, I was feeling more and more fretful.

And then feeling cornered and down to my last and when all seemed to be lost, the cavalry came charging in the shape of Lindsay Henson, fast shooting and immediately reassuring. HMRC were sent scurrying away for cover, hiding behind their rule books knowing they had met their match. The result? A small tax bill, a tiny bit of interest and no more questions.

I now sleep peacefully at night knowing that if they do ever call, Lindsay is right behind me. Lindsay has the exceptional qualities of being fiercely protective, amazingly sharp and warm and cuddly at the same time.

Guy Bolam
Bolam Rose
Financial Advisers

"The art of taxation consists of plucking the goose so as to obtain the largest possible amount of feathers with the smallest possible amount of hissing.

Jean B. Colbert

chapter 1
Insider savings

Having many years of experience on both sides of the fence, I can say with some authority that it is virtually impossible to escape the taxman's net, particularly as he can, in some cases, go back and collect tax for the previous 20 years. This book gives tips on how to save tax, but also on how to save money on unnecessary interest, surcharges and penalties by getting the paperwork right at the right time. It can also save you money on expensive accountancy advice by giving some DIY tips for the brave amongst you.

Many of the tips are tactical ones on how to deal with HMRC or how to understand the system, as it's far from simple to navigate and is known as one of the most complex tax systems in the world. Believe it or not, the taxman only wants you to pay the right amount of tax and only one in three of us does this via an annual tax return. There are two ways of saving tax—by 'tax avoidance' and 'tax evasion'—and the difference between them is the thickness of the prison walls!

The legal route

Tax avoidance is legal: you are utilising the tax regime to your own advantage, to reduce the amount of tax payable, by means that are within the law.

A definite no no

Tax evasion, by contrast, is what HMRC are out to catch and is what keeps me in a job! It is those efforts by individuals or companies to evade tax by illegal means, often by the deliberate misrepresentation or concealment of the true state of their affairs to reduce their tax liability... and there's a lot of it about!

What's it all about?

The United Kingdom comprises England, Scotland, Wales and Northern Ireland, together with most of the small islands around the British coast. The Channel Islands, the Isle of Man and the Republic of Ireland are not part of the UK for tax purposes.

The Income Tax year runs from 6 April to the following 5 April. In common with many countries, the UK may require taxpayers to file an annual return of taxable income and gains, and self assess the tax due. There are fixed filing and payment dates.

Many employees pay all their tax through payroll withholding under PAYE and are not required to file a tax return. However, the more complicated your tax position, the more likely you will have to file a return. If you need to file your own tax return, but have not been sent one to complete, you should request one from HMRC by 5 October following the tax year. It's your responsibility, not theirs!

Tax residents receive an annual tax-free personal allowance, and this increases annually. Tax is not due until your taxable income exceeds this amount.

If you are tax resident for only part of the UK tax year, you will nevertheless receive your full annual tax-free personal allowance. If you are non-resident in the UK, you will only be entitled to a personal allowance if you are a citizen of the Commonwealth or a citizen of a Member country of the European Economic Area or if you are entitled to the allowance under specific double tax treaty provisions which cover personal allowances.

Your tax home

Whilst we all know where we live, with Europe increasingly opening up to us for work and second homes, the way the taxman views us can have a dramatic effect on what tax we pay. In simple terms use the following tips as a guide to your residency for tax:

Resident

- If you're in the UK for 183 days or more in a tax year, you're a 'resident' for that year for tax purposes.
- If you come to live in the UK permanently or to remain for three years or more you're resident from the date of arrival.
- You're also treated as resident if you're in the UK for an average of 91 days or more in a tax year (worked out over a maximum of four consecutive tax years.)

Ordinarily resident

- If you're resident in the UK year after year you will normally be treated as 'ordinarily resident'.
- You're treated as ordinarily resident in the UK from the date you arrive if it's clear that you intend to stay for at least three years.

Confused? That's normal! So in this ever changing-world, if you're affected grab 10 minutes with a friendly accountant!

Domicile

- Your domicile is normally acquired at birth, and this is a general law concept covering a range of factors. Your domicile of origin at birth is normally that of your father – and it is very difficult to change this. A domicile of choice means severing all ties with the UK, involving closing UK bank accounts, selling UK assets and even organising your funeral abroad.

TACTICAL TIP

Every day counts! Days spent in and out of the UK are crucial in determining your tax liability, as are your habits and the nature of your employment. These days, passports are seldom stamped as evidence of travel, so retain all travel documents, tickets, vouchers, receipts, credit card and bank statements, proving your absence abroad.

Domicile dilemma

Your domicile status has a profound effect on your tax affairs – both for Income Tax (IT) and Inheritance Tax (IHT). If you were born overseas but now live in the UK you could be non-domiciled. If you have income arising overseas, seek the advice of a tax specialist to help maximise any tax advantages. And it's all change in 2008, as the government tackle head on non-doms resident in Britain. Those resident in Britain for more than 7 out of the last 10 tax years, could face paying a flat £30,000 p.a, lose out on personal IT and Capital Gains Tax (CGT) allowances or, possibly for the first time, they may start to pay UK tax on their overseas income, like the rest of the UK domiciled residents do, so watch this space!

Even if you are no longer a British resident, it is extremely difficult to escape IHT. Anyone domiciled in Britain must pay UK tax at 40% on worldwide assets above the annual threshold. If you are granted a new domicile of choice, it takes three years for the loss of UK domicile to become effective for IHT purposes.

Saying goodbye

Be sure to tell the Revenue if you are leaving the UK and complete form P85 to claim any tax repayment due. This will help them decide your residence and whether you will still need to complete a tax return. On your return you will fill out form P86 to complete the picture for them and re-join the club.

Penny pinching from pensions

Sadly, state pensions and any company or personal pensions are taxable. State pensions are paid without tax deducted, but company and personal pensions usually have tax taken off first. HMRC are automatically notified when you start getting your state pension, but there's often a delay. It's a good idea to tell them yourself in advance, to avoid getting behind with any tax payments.

The good news is, if your income, including your state pension, is less than your personal tax-free allowances, then you won't pay tax on your state pension. If your total income exceeds your tax allowances, you'll have to pay tax on your state pension. This is collected from your other income through your code number — making the tax paid seem extraordinarily high, a pensioner's usual gripe. So check your tax code notice to make sure it shows the amount of state pension you'll actually get for the current year and contact the tax office if it's wrong.

TOP TIP

The taxman has a bad memory and may forget your birthday. Six months before your 65th, give him a call to ensure he puts your higher age-related allowances in your code number.

Help the aged

When you are over 65 the personal allowances go up and are increased further when you reach 75. But watch as these are restricted if your income exceeds certain limits (see *Free advice* on page 20). With good planning married couples can equalise income or invest wisely to get the most from their allowances.

What a relief

One of the greatest remaining breaks is that the money you pay into a pension still qualifies for tax relief at your highest rate – whether it's a personal pension or through your employer's scheme.

Starting early

Parents, grandparents or even godparents can pay into a stakeholder pension for a newborn baby. Currently by paying £2,808 net, the fund swells by £3,600, courtesy of the taxman. They can repeat it each year and it works for someone of any age. It is, however, a long-term investment as the child cannot touch it until age 50. You may, therefore, not be around to see them thank you for it!

Pension time bomb

- Most of us are guilty of massively overestimating the true value of our expected retirement income. We want to maintain our lifestyles but may have to work longer to do so. We all love to spend, spend, spend to keep up in this celebrity-mad world, and whilst this may help reduce the IHT bill, the foreign holidays and plasma TVs we all deem indispensable inevitably restrict what we can put aside for the future.

- The good news is we are living longer with more and more passing the 100 mark.

- The not-so-good news is the value of the state pension has fallen to under 20% of average earnings.

- Work patterns are changing as redundancy, short-term contracts, sabbaticals, and maternity leave seriously limit continuous employment.

- Pension confidence has been diminished due to pension mis-selling, bad publicity, falling rates and the collapse of final salary schemes.

- But consumer borrowing to fund luxury goods continues to climb.

Take advice, life's about choice and the choice is yours. Obtain a state pension forecast by sending off form BR19 – it will tell you what sums to expect and how to increase it, possibly by voluntary contributions.

Tax in a nutshell

Income Tax
Charged on earnings, pensions, profits from self-employment, and savings income.

National Insurance
Paid by employees, employers and the self-employed – but not once you reach pensionable age (65 for men, 60 for women).

Capital Gains Tax
Payable on the profit you make on selling assets – like property.

Inheritance Tax
Generally payable on everything you own at the date you die less what you owe, over an annual threshold, with some exceptions.

Corporation Tax
Paid on company profits.

Value Added Tax (V.A.T.)
A tax on goods and services.

Stamp duty
Paid on property transactions and stock market deals.

Call him to account

If you use an accountant, don't be afraid to query their bill or ask for a breakdown. You may get a reduction – especially if you kept clear and accurate records for him.

Punitive penalties

There's no escape from automatic penalties for late tax return filing. Initially it's £100 – whether you owe £100 and file one day late or £100,000 and file three months late. Don't let the fine catch you – it can be out of all proportion to the crime. The only get-out-of-jail card is that if you owe less than £100, the penalty is restricted to that amount.

Free advice

Everyone, from the day they are born, is entitled to tax free IT and CGT allowances. Larger accountants produce free, handy, pocket-sized cards packed full of useful tax data, so pop in and pick one up. For specific queries, most accountants are willing to give new potential customers half an hour's free advice. Make an appointment to pick their brains and if they can save you serious amounts of time or money – sign up, after negotiating a fair price of course!

Or make the taxman work. Free leaflets, booklets and help sheets are available from HMRC online or by a telephone order. Or 'phone him or write. It's not as effective as meeting him face to face however and certainly not as quick. In matters of complexity, don't rely on their pamphlets – they are very general. Keep a copy of any letters you send, and if calling, note the officer's name and the date and time of the call.

Don't rely on the 'man in the pub' for advice, far better to wait for the taxman's reply however long it takes! If you do manage to arrange a personal appointment – take along your passport or photo driver's licence and a recent utility bill as they may check you are who you say you are!

Get online

File your tax return online and get an immediate acknowledgement of its receipt. You can then log on to view your account – showing what's due and when.

Fast cash

If you know you are due a tax repayment, submit your return over the Internet. The repayment is likely to be issued more promptly than for paper returns, which have to be manually input, by a human, in the tax office. Online, there's less chance for the taxman to intercept it and change his mind. Remember to enter your bank account details and you'll probably find the repayment turns up in your account before the explanatory paperwork lands on your mat.

Excuses, excuses

You may think that you have a reasonable excuse for the late filing of your return, but the taxman thinks otherwise. The law does not define reasonable excuse and according to the taxman, a reasonable excuse can only exist where "an exceptional event beyond the control of the taxpayer prevented completion and return of the tax return by the due date". Death may be accepted but a last minute dash to Dubai will not!

Don't shoot the messenger

Failure by your tax adviser to submit your return by the deadline would not normally be accepted as a reasonable excuse. In the taxman's eyes, it is the responsibility of each taxpayer to ensure returns are made on time and that they are complete and correct.

In the frame

The majority of tax enquiries (previously called investigations) are not generated at random. Your returns are 'screened' to identify those that contain likely material for further questioning. (More on this in chapter 5.) The taxman can't solve any problems he has with your return alone, but under self-assessment rules, he can't request any information from you without formally opening an enquiry. Result: Enquiry opened even if the answer he gets shows that it wasn't necessary.

Look back

Keep a copy of your tax returns and accompanying information and notes every year. While completing your return, compare it with last year's form. Satisfy yourself you can explain any variances in the figures and if these are substantial write an explanation in the "additional information" box. Tell him about relevant changes in circumstances, cessations or commencements of income sources, with full details. The additional information box will only be read if your case is being considered for enquiry. That's when what you've recorded could deselect you from further hassle.

More or less

HMRC will tell you they don't want your paper accounts, accompanying letters or explanations stapling to the return as it hampers their processing system. Ignore them. Send in your additional information with the tax return. That way you could reduce your chances of an enquiry being opened, just to get at what your additional information explains. But write your unique tax reference (UTR) prominently on all enclosures, as it's not unknown for them to go missing when undergoing the bulk 'process now, check later' system in some distant central processing department.

Knock, knock – who's there?

A visit to your local tax office to sort out a problem is not as easy as it used to be. Many are closing down or merging with others so don't be surprised to see your case being handled hundreds of miles away.

NI No

An NI number is issued to UK residents automatically just before their 16th birthday providing that their parents have claimed child benefit. People coming into the UK may need to apply for one. The reason that an NI number is important is that it is unique to you and records your earnings for NI and benefits purposes. Also HMRC's PAYE computer system is based around NI numbers.

Total recall

Memorise your NI number. It consists of two letters followed by six numbers and then either an A, B, C or D. It's the only one you will get from age 16, and is needed to access your tax records. Don't overpay on NICs.

If you are both employed and self-employed, you may well be paying above the maximum in NICs. The relevant HMRC department in Newcastle will help you decide whether you are paying too much and arrange for a deferment or refund. The difficult bit is getting through to them on the phone! Once you do it's quite simple to sort.

Clearing the CGT minefield

Tax is constantly changing with radical alteration to CGT from 6th April 2008. Up until then the regime involved an extremely complicated combination of reliefs and deductions, often favourable to entrepreneurs. Simplification seldom occurs in tax (why is simplification such a long word I ask myself?) and the Chancellor's original intention to make CGT less complex, was met with screams of protest from business owners who quite rightly spotted a potential 80% hike in tax on the sale of their firms.

Quick tip

NO CHANGE THERE
The CGT changes only affect individuals and trustees. Companies have never had taper relief and will continue to benefit from indexation allowance.

So what's the upshot?

- A flat rate of 18%.
- Taper relief and indexation allowance abolished.
- 'Entrepreneurs' relief allowing business owners with a stake of more than 5%, to pay only 10% CGT on gains up to £1m – but remember, this is a lifetime.
- Winners include higher-raters selling second homes or buy-to-lets.
- The annual CGT tax-free allowance remains so make good use of it.

Win or lose, the change will affect your assets, pocket and decisions. It's worth looking at the big picture and remembering that sometimes there's more to life than cutting your tax bills.

All your worldly goods

A painting is an example of a "chattel", and as such, is exempt from CGT if it is sold for less than £6,000. If it is sold for more than £6,000, CGT is relevant. The maximum chargeable gain is based on 5/3rds of the difference between the sale proceeds and £6,000.

If sold for £12,000, the maximum gain would be 5/3rds times £6,000, which is £10,000. Compare this figure to the actual gain (proceeds less costs). As results vary, you return the lower resultant gain. If the chattel is jointly owned, however, each owner is entitled to the £6,000 exemption, so if you make your wife a joint owner of the painting before you sell it, you will each be exempt on your £6,000 share of the sale proceeds.

eBay beware

The taxman is most definitely chasing people who sell things on eBay, and similar sites, to demand tax. So should you expect a knock on the door from him?

The first question to ask yourself is whether you are "trading" or not. There are certain badges of trade which will help you decide:

- Are you buying and selling with a view to a profit?
- Are you buying and selling regularly?
- Are your activities connected with another trade you run? E.g. you buy and sell rugs on eBay, and also run a carpet shop.
- Do you modify things you buy in order to make them more valuable? Such as buying wool and knitting jumpers?
- Do you sell in a businesslike fashion? E.g. bulk-buy and sell smaller lots.
- Do you borrow money for goods and sell them to repay the loan?
- Do you turn the items over rapidly?

No one answer will be conclusive, but be honest and you will get a feel for whether you are trading or not. It's like the elephant – difficult to describe, but unmistakable when it's in the front room!

Time's up

A great tip for throwing the book at HMRC is to quote their own Extra Statutory Concession A19 at them:

"Giving up tax where there are Revenue delays in using information".

Arrears of IT or CGT may be given up if they result from HMRC's failure to make proper and timely use of information supplied by:

- You the taxpayer about your income, gains or personal circumstances.
- An employer, where the information affects someone's coding.
- The DWP about State Pensions, Disability or Widows Pensions.

Tax will normally be "given up" only where the taxpayer:

- Was notified of the arrears more than 12 months after the end of the tax year in which HMRC received the information indicating that more tax was due.
- Was notified of an over-repayment after the end of the tax year following the year in which the repayment was made.
- Could reasonably have believed that his tax affairs were in order.
- There are other exceptional circumstances too, so if you fall victim to Revenue delay, don't be shy, they might try to wriggle out of it, but quoting the above rules may get your arrears written off!

The civil list

The 2004 Civil Partnership Act resulted in tax breaks mainly affecting IHT and CGT. So what attracted so many high-profile gay celebrities to it and what's it all about?

- It's for two people of the same sex.
- Formed when they register before a civil partnership registrar and two witnesses.
- With no religious ceremony and not on religious premises.
- For over 18s in England and Wales (or over 16 with parental consent).
- Not for those already in a partnership/married.
- It ends on death, dissolution or annulment.
- Court can issue a dissolution order on breakdown, on similar terms to divorce or separation orders.
- Nullity order issued if void e.g. one party is pregnant by another at registration date. Nullity grounds do not include non-consummation.
- Presumption of death order available with presumption of death after 7 years absence.
- Ability to leave assets IHT-free.
- IHT planning as for spouses.
- IHT tax-free transfers.
- CGT inter-partner transfers at 'no gains/no loss'.
- Utilise annual exemptions for CGT.
- Connected persons rules apply.
- Equalise investment income to lower-rate partner.

A happy tax life

Marriage matters big time for the capital taxes—CGT and IHT—with big savings to be made. However it takes communication, honesty and trust to get it right. OK I've lost a few of you already! No ladies, you don't have to tell him how much you spend on clothes but you will have to divulge the property and shares you own. So unless you're a member of the silent minority read on.

Each spouse has an annual allowance for Capital Gains Tax purposes up to which all gains you make on selling or transferring assets are tax free. It makes sound financial sense to 'divvie' up the assets which are sitting on potential gains, so that you utilise both annual exemptions and so double up the tax saving.

Cash back

Everyone living in the UK can receive some income before tax has to be paid. If your income is below that limit and you have money in a bank or building society you could automatically be paying tax on your interest when you don't have to. There's a fortune sitting in HMRC's coffers and you may be entitled to it!

But beware if it involves gifts of money to children, where:

* Your child's account includes money that was a gift from you.
* Your gifts produce more than £100 gross interest a tax year.

Your child cannot have interest paid without tax taken off and cannot claim any tax back. The interest is treated as yours and must be declared on your tax return.

Otherwise, complete form R85 for each bank or building society to receive your interest tax-free. Claim back any tax you have suffered in error for the previous six years by making a repayment claim on form R40. Don't be frightened to claim and it's never too small to bother with – it's yours.

Free and easy

H M Revenue and Customs' own web site is an easy to navigate free guide to a mind-boggling number of taxes and benefits which come under their remit. However you may care to note the Revenue's promise enshrined on its own home page that "we are here to ensure the correct tax is paid at the right time, whether this relates to payment of taxes received by the department or entitlement to benefits paid".

Many people do not pay the right amount of tax or receive the benefits due, as borne out by the frequent complaints to the department. So visit their web site and check that you are up to date from their "what's new" section and look inside their own internal instruction manuals to ensure you are paying what's due – no more, no less.

The carrot and stick summary

As the self-assessment years have gone by, the sticks have far outweighed the carrots in the tax system, with interest, penalties, and surcharges charged automatically for even minor misdemeanours. Make the most of this bunch of tax and stress-saving carrots while they are still there for the picking.

Ten timely tax tips

1. Max up your pension contributions pre 5th April to gain generous tax relief.

2. An ISA's nicer. Individual Savings Accounts are great for tax-free savings (but count for IHT).

3. Use your other half. A higher rate taxpayer can save tax by transferring money into a lower earning—or non-earning—spouse or civil partner's name.

4. Make a will. It's the only way to be sure your loved ones don't miss out on their inheritance, and limit tax paid on your estate. (See Chapter 3.)

5. Check your code number, or you could be paying over the odds. (See Chapter 8.)

6. Rent a room. Many people raise extra Income Tax-free by renting out a room in their home. (See Chapter 2.)

7. Negotiate a reduced price with house vendor to drop the price below stamp duty thresholds.

8. Company car? Broadly speaking, the smaller the vehicle, the less tax you pay.

9. Make sure you take full advantage of your annual CGT allowance.

10. Kids get their own personal tax and CGT allowances and you can set up tax-efficient trusts for children or grandchildren.

> " Like mothers, taxes are often misunderstood, but seldom forgotten. "

Lord Bramwell

chapter 2
Home & away

Tax queries around 'bricks and mortar' make up possibly the largest segment of an adviser's daily work. Stock market and pension scares encouraged many to invest in buy-to-let properties, holiday homes and commercial premises. Of course our own family homes represent the biggest investment most of us will ever make and apart from the stamp duty on acquisition and its value for IHT when we die, the taxman largely leaves us alone to cash in on whatever equity we can make on it. Run a business from it or buy a second home and he will want to know. So be aware of the pitfalls as well as the advantages and never try to hide a property from the taxman's eyes as he has many ways of tracking you down, as you will see from the final chapter.

Good connections

Whether you are "connected" in the eyes of the Revenue can seriously affect your tax liabilities so here's a guide to who you are connected with:

- Your husband or wife or civil partner.
- Your brothers and sisters and your spouse's or civil partner's brothers and sisters.
- Your parents, grandparents and other ancestors and your spouse's or civil partner's parents, grandparents or other ancestors.

- Your children and other lineal descendants and your spouses or civil partner's children and other lineal descendants.

- The husbands or wives or civil partners of any of the relatives listed above.

- Your business partners and their relatives, together with the husbands and wives or civil partners of those partners, except for genuine commercial acquisitions or disposals of partnership assets.

- Any company that you control, either by yourself or with any of the persons listed above.

- The trustees of a settlement of which you, or any living individual who is connected with you, are the settler.

Calling all landlords

Let out property and receive rent and this is treated for tax purposes as if you are running a rental business. It doesn't matter if you let just one small flat or many different properties, for tax they will all be treated as a single business. Rent (after expenses have been deducted) is regarded as part of your total UK income.

Properties that you let out for people to live in as their home count as 'residential lettings' and are treated differently from furnished UK holiday lettings. If you let property abroad, you may have to pay UK tax on the rental income. Let your home while you live somewhere else and your profits are taxed in the same way as for your residential investment lettings.

Rents – what can you claim?

Effectively all receipts and expenses can be lumped together. This includes the letting of furnished or unfurnished property. (Income from furnished holiday lettings is calculated separately). The allowable deductions shown below are expenses wholly and exclusively incurred for the purposes of the business.

1. Travel and rent collection

   The cost of business travel to and from the let property is allowable, as is the cost of rent collection for properties let on a commercial basis.

2. Interest

   Payable on loans to buy land, or property, or to fund repairs, improvements or alterations.

3. Unpaid rent

   You can deduct a debt that is irrecoverable.

4. Legal expenses

   Here you must differentiate between capital and revenue expenditure, i.e. the costs of the purchase of the property or the first lease are capital and not allowable but the costs of renewing leases for less than 50 years are allowable. Thus a series of 6 monthly, short hold tenancies, are allowable.

5. Repairs

   Again repairs must distinguish capital from revenue. Examples of common repairs, which are normally deductible in computing your rental profits (i.e. revenue expenditure) are:

- Painting and decorating.
- Cleaning.
- Damp and rot treatment.
- Mending broken windows, doors, furniture, cookers, etc.
- Re-pointing brickwork.
- Repairing roof slates, flashing, and gutters.

Examples of capital expenditure are:

- Expenditure that adds to or improves your property, e.g. converting an outbuilding to holiday accommodation.
- The cost of refurbishing or repairing a property you bought in a derelict state.
- The cost of a completely new building.
- Access roads and car parks.

The difference between what is capital expenditure and allowable revenue expenses, is a minefield and if you are unsure consult a professional adviser or your tax office – the former may well cost you, however the latter might throw up a variety of opinions (if my experience is anything to go by) so always get it in writing.

6. Rent, rates, council tax and insurance

Allowable expenses include:

- Rents you pay to a landlord for property you are subletting.
- Business rates, council tax, ground rents.
- Insurance for buildings and contents.
- Insurance against loss of rents.

7. **Bad and doubtful debts**
- Debts clearly irrecoverable.
- Doubtful debts estimated to be irrecoverable, provided you have a solid reason for thinking the debt is likely to be bad and have taken all reasonable steps to recover it.

8. **Services provided**
   If you include services under the terms of the lease as ordinary incidents of letting they are deductible, i.e. cleaning, gardening.

9. **Advertising**
   E.g. for new tenants.

10. **Wear and tear allowances for furnished residential property**
    Where you let a residential property furnished, Capital Allowances cannot be claimed for furniture or fixtures but you are able to claim either:

- An annual wear and tear allowance of 10% of the net rents (being the rents received less council tax, water and sewerage rates etc.)

    or

- The net cost of replacing a particular item of furniture, but not the cost of the original purchases on the "renewals basis". This covers similar items as the 10% wear and tear allowance such as:
- Beds and suites.
- Televisions.
- Fridges and freezers.

- Carpets and curtains.
- Bed linen and towels.
- Crockery and cutlery.

The entitlement to the 10% deduction can be claimed automatically if your let property is genuinely furnished, that is, includes everyday items such as a bed, chairs, tables, cooker, etc. It does not depend upon items being provided every year. The great advantage is that it is simple to calculate and you get the deduction from the start, whereas the 'renewals basis' only gives relief when you replace the initial furnishings.

Departing these shores

Your escape to the sun will not mean you escape the taxman's clutches. If your UK rent exceeds £5,200 a year, any letting agent you engage is duty bound to deduct the basic rate of tax from your rents.

But you can apply to HMRC to receive all your rents in full without deduction of tax under the Non-Resident Landlord Scheme if:

- Your UK tax affairs are up to date;
- You have never had any UK tax obligations;
- You don't have to pay UK Income Tax.

In these circumstances you will be responsible for filling in your own return and paying up.

Holiday lets

Distinctly advantageous over other lettings, namely allowing loss relief and Capital Gains Tax reliefs.

The tests are basically that each tax year the property must be:

- In the UK.
- Furnished and available for immediate occupation.
- Let at a commercial rent.
- Available for holiday letting on a commercial basis for 140 days or more.
- Let for at least 70 days.
- Not occupied for more than 31 days by the same person in a 7-month period.

Wedded to your assets

When a married couple or civil partners live together, the transfer of assets between them is treated as giving rise to neither gain nor loss. This still applies in the year of separation which is a very important tax planning point. OK, it's not always possible to plan a date of separation and tax is likely to be the last thing on your mind at this traumatic time, but when both parties often need every penny they can get, it's foolish to hand over a big chunk to Mr Taxman – particularly as your lawyers will have already reduced the pot substantially!

Couples have until the 5th April following the date of separation to transfer assets, e.g. property, shares, to each other tax free. In its extreme 6th April is the ideal date giving you 12 months to divide up the assets, whereas 24th March gives you only 12 days!

Flying the nest, feathering their own

Gap year has flown by, home constraints look unappealing, university beckons. If circumstances allow, rather than rent rooms, try to arrange for your children to purchase their own property. Make sure it is in their name by obtaining a mortgage in their name with you guaranteeing the payments if necessary. If they let part to their friends, the whole exercise is a tax planning dream. Potentially there is unlikely to be any tax on the rental income after deducting mortgage interest, décor, repairs, etc. On its sale, it is their main residence and probably fully exempt from CGT. Also rent-a-room relief would be relevant – per 'the lodger dodger' tip.

Just think, they are on the property ladder and any equity they build up may well pay off the student debts at the end of the degree! Or maybe not! Either way it may instil some sense of responsibility in them even if it's dad who has to cut the grass and mum who fills the freezer.

The lodger dodger

HMRC still allow a tax efficient scheme useful for those living in university cities with a high student population, who have spare rooms and want to make them pay. Visions of 'Rigsby-like' situations come to mind (for those of you who remember Rising Damp!). If you let furnished rooms in your own home and the income is less than £4,250 the income is not taxable. Landlords do not need to own the property, only live in it, so it can apply to tenants sub-letting a room. The scheme does not apply however to homes converted into separate flats or bed sits.

The scheme's a simple way of receiving up to £4,250 rent a year without the need for paperwork, accounts or tax! One downside of the Rent-a-Room Scheme is that landlords cannot claim any expenses relating to the letting, such as insurance, or repairs. Some may be better off declaring all their letting income and claiming the expenses.

The choice is yours, but be aware that:

- It must be furnished – no relief for unfurnished accommodation.
- Landlords must live on the premises.
- Your lease or mortgage must allow it.
- Your home insurance polices must be changed.
- Proof of the rents received—preferably a rent book—should be kept.
- If a room is let jointly (say by husband and wife) the limit is £2,125 each.

TACTICAL TIP

The scheme allows two ways to work out your tax if your receipts exceed the exemption limits. Compare the income you are left with after your expenses with the amount of your receipts above £4,250 (or £2,125 if letting jointly) and elect for the resultant lesser tax treatment to apply.

Double, double, avoiding trouble

We all know that our private homes are free of CGT in an ideal world, allowing us to move up the property ladder, hopefully building up equity.

But where a person owns and occupies two properties, it is important to consider carefully which property should be the main residence and an election made accordingly. For example, the current main residence could well be the family Lincolnshire cottage which does not have the same capital appreciation as the Monday to Friday London penthouse. Both are used as homes and it would be wise to elect for the "greater gain" to be exempt, i.e. probably the London flat. A timely election, as above, must be made within two years but it can be changed from time to time as circumstances alter. That is, within two years of the start of the period when it first becomes necessary to decide which of your two or more homes is the main one.

Electing for a second home to be your main residence, even for a short period of time before switching it back, will give you the final three years of ownership free of CGT when it is sold, with little effect on the taxation of property number one.

As soon as a second property has been purchased an election should be made, but each property must be a residence, ownership alone is not sufficient! Proof of this could be – ensuring postal communications (your tax returns!) go to the address, paying council tax and utility bills, and completing the electoral roll forms. A practical tip is to take photos of family life there and date them – after all the camera never lies!

Good manors

Tax is due on the sale of a second home, but make sure it is registered in two names from the start, to benefit from two CGT annual exemptions.

Business beware

You might assume the profit on your home is free from CGT, but you may be left exposed to a large bill if you use the home partly for your business. Note down the dates and rooms involved, taking photos if to ensure you are taxed fairly. Tax is charged when you use a part of the house exclusively for the business, eg. extension used as a store or workshop. Tax will not apply if you are merely typing the odd letter whilst sat at the kitchen table.

Offloading the land

If cutting the grass in your large garden gets too much for you, you can sell off part of the "permitted area" attached to your home of up to 0.5 hectares (about an acre) without selling the property itself, and not pay CGT on the profit. Interested? Call an accountant in advance to get peace of mind!

Best kept secrets

By re-mortgaging rental properties up to 100% of their original purchase price or introducing your home into the rental portfolio at it's market value and re-financing up to that value, you can use the funds for absolutely anything and claim a tax deduction in your rental accounts. Now the secret's out!

DIY builders beware

A DIY home-build is a popular way to put more profit in your pocket, courtesy of the Vatman! Most of the construction work can be billed VAT free and VAT re-claimed at the end on virtually all materials and services. You can only make one VAT re-claim after the construction is finished and it may be around 3 months before you see the money in your bank. It will amount to a few thousand and be handy for funding that necessary stress-busting holiday away from the nightmare of a self-build project.

Summary

The tax tips around property generally focus on profits. Of course losses can and do occur, but live in a property for a few years and you're very likely to come into the biggest tax-free windfall of your life. The downside for some, possibly in a time of serious recession, is that there's no tax relief on a loss on selling your own home.

Be tax wise:

- Plan ahead.

- Take advice.

- Keep records.

- Consider all parties and joint ownership.

- Get the legal paperwork right.

- Don't try to conceal anything from the taxman.

Tax trivia

- In 1799 Income Tax was introduced to fund the war with France against Napoleon.

- At the start of World War I in 1914, the standard rate of tax was 6% and produced Income Tax of £44 million for the exchequer plus £3m in super tax. By 1918 the rate had risen to 30% in order to bring in £275m in Income Tax and £736m in super tax – what a difference a war makes.

- Due to the growing number of workers during World War II, there was a need for an efficient method of tax collection, so PAYE was introduced in 1944 – some things never change!

- Queen Elizabeth II elected to pay tax on her income in a move to bring the monarchy closer to the people in 1992 – oh, to have the choice!

- Surtax, a super tax, was introduced by Lloyd George in 1909 and not abolished until 1973, hence the prevalence of celebrity tax exiles.

- Despite the fight for women's financial independence and equality in tax, beginning in 1882 with the Married Woman's Property Act, married women were not taxed independently until 1990. Prior to this her income was treated as part of her husband's – surely that should be the other way round!

> **In this world nothing can be said to be certain – except death and taxes.**

Benjamin Franklin

chapter 3
The death trap

Statistics may show that only about 6% of death estates come into Inheritance Tax, but with property prices hitting all time highs, particularly in London and the South East, more and more ordinary taxpayers are facing the IHT time bomb, as their homes push them over the threshold and into the pool of contributors to the £4 billion a year in tax it raises.

So it's not just footballer's wives and landed gentry being brought into the IHT net but people like you and me – IHT is seen as a bigger UK growth area than the rise of the hi-visibility jacket!

A voluntary tax

Inheritance Tax is a tax that's sometimes payable on your 'estate'. Broadly speaking this is everything you own at the time of your death, less what you owe. It's also sometimes payable on assets you gave during your lifetime. Assets include things like property, possessions, money, and investments.

Not everyone pays IHT on death, by definition it's the one tax you don't pay personally! It stands at a flat rate of 40% and only applies if the value of the net estate exceeds the threshold. So avoid it – learn to 'SKI' and 'Spend the Kids Inheritance'!

All change

October 2007 saw a fundamental change relating to IHT allowances. The IHT threshold, normally rising annually, is also known as the nil rate band. There was no change to the position whereby assets can be left to a spouse or civil partner free of IHT (with the non-domiciled exception).

TOP TIP

These provisions apply to all survivors of a marriage or civil partnership who themselves die after 9 October 2007, irrespective of when their partners died, i.e. to those who are already widowed. But take care – anyone widowed twice cannot use more than one extra total IHT threshold amount. Claims only need to be made on the death of the surviving spouse so keep a record of the unused proportion of the deceased's nil rate band for future reference.

In the past everyone benefited from their own individual IHT allowance and everything above this tax-free band was taxable at 40%. At a stroke all that changed, to allow married couples and civil partners to transfer any unused nil rate band down to their surviving spouse/partner, thus potentially doubling up the value of their IHT allowances. Previously it was possible to maximise both IHT thresholds, to allow couples to minimise IHT by doubling up on the two tax free bands, but this relied upon nil rate band trust planning in wills, which could be costly and complicated.

Now, save on these costs under the new rules and achieve the same result – when the first partner dies his or her IHT allowance automatically passes to the survivor.

The losers

The new rules do not apply to:

- Unmarried couples who live together.
- Same sex couples who are not in a legal civil partnership.
- Brothers and sisters who live together.
- Divorcees.
- Single people.

They are all left in the same position as before, as are those couples who have already drawn up wills establishing discretionary trusts using their nil-rate bands (effectively already allowing them both to use their individual IHT allowances). If you already have a trust written in your will do not panic. If you are both still alive there's plenty of time to decide whether to implement it or add simple codicils to your wills.

Life line

To make it easier for you to work out how much of a deceased spouse's nil rate band remains available when a surviving spouse subsequently dies, HMRC has published "nil rate band" tables for IHT (and its predecessor taxes), for all years from August 1914 to the present date.

Visit www.hmrc.gov.uk/cto/customerguide/page15.htm

Ten tips to reduce IHT

1. **Plan in advance**
   Where do you want your money to go and why? Many people cannot easily give away assets – they trust their children, but not always their kids' spouses!

2. **Make a will**
   A will makes it clear who should get what. It will stop assets being divided under the rules of intestacy, where even spouses are not guaranteed to inherit everything. It can also be a method of reducing an IHT bill too.

3. **Minimise your estate**
   You cannot be taxed on money that was never yours. So ensure that as much as possible is outside your estate.

4. **Be married or in a civil partnership**
   Anything you pass on to a spouse or civil partner, even if above the threshold, is free of IHT if you are both domiciled in the UK.

5. **Consider your home**
   For many, your home will be your biggest asset. The Government has clamped down on schemes to get around the 'gifts with reservation' rules. These allowed people to give away homes, but still live in them. Now, Income Tax can be charged for living rent-free in a home you once owned. If they don't get you one way, they'll get you another!

6. Investments

   Some investments are given favourable treatment for IHT purposes, including shares in unquoted businesses, woodlands, farms and farmland. Many shares on the Alternative Investment Market also qualify for relief.

7. Explore trusts

   Aside from will trusts, several others can help in estate planning. Depending on the type you choose, it can still be possible to enjoy an income from money paid into trust, even though you are no longer the legal owner of that money – but take specialist advice.

8. Pay in instalments

   An option is to estimate how big an IHT bill your heirs face and then arrange insurance to cover part or all of it. Whole-of-life insurance written under trust can provide a lump sum on death that is outside an estate.

9. Spend it

   Throw off the shackles, spend it and enjoy yourself.

10. Use annual allowances

    Giving away money will reduce your estate, but will not cut the liability immediately. You have to survive for seven years for most gifts to escape the IHT net.

Tenants in common

'Tenants in Common' has long been known as a vehicle to get around the taxman and reduce IHT. Taking the new rules into account, if you still need to consider this, all you need to do is change the ownership of your home from joint names to being tenants in common. If you own your home as joint tenants then both of you own the whole of the property, so when one partner dies, the other automatically becomes the sole owner of the home. With tenants in common, you each own a share of the property, typically split 50/50.

There is no IHT to pay on assets willed between husband and wife, so the surviving partner does not have to pay IHT. But when the second partner dies, those who inherit the estate, typically the children, would have to pay IHT at 40% on any assets over the nil-rate band levels.

By splitting the home in two, the half belonging to the first partner to die could be passed straight onto their children or designated beneficiary. When the second partner dies, their half is then passed on. It's not all plain sailing as it relies on a lot of trust between you and your offspring. Make the switch through someone having expert knowledge of wills and trusts. The new rules explained above have however, reduced the need for this type of arrangement for some.

The will won't wait

If you are one of the 27 million people in England and Wales who does not have a will you are effectively gambling with your loved ones' lives. Unmarried couples can be particularly vulnerable as the IHT laws fail to protect a surviving partner (unless a legal civil partnership exists), who can lose property, possessions and cash.

Appoint guardians, often family members, for any children in the event that you both pre-decease them.

A will is the essential way to ensure that your estate is shared out exactly as you want it to be and should prevent the break out of family rows.

Without one, rules for sharing out your estate—called the Laws of Intestacy—could mean your money going to family members who may not need it, or your unmarried partner receiving nothing at all.

Power of attorney

It is now no longer possible to create an "Enduring Power of Attorney" but those currently in existence will remain legally binding. Instead a new "Lasting Power of Attorney" is required which must be registered with the Public Guardian.

Visit www.guardianship.gov.uk

Ten tips for a perfect will

1. **Choose who draws up your will wisely**
   You can make your own will using a DIY kit available from the local stationers but the process is full of pitfalls, and errors are easy to make.

2. **Choose your executors well**
   Executors are responsible for dealing with your estate in accordance with your instructions after you have died. It is a responsible and demanding role, so don't forget to check that they are happy to take it on.

3. **Appoint a substitute**
   If you are married, you will probably want your spouse to be your executor, but don't make them your sole executor. If you both died together, neither of you would have an executor living so always appoint a default executor as a fallback position.

4. **Appoint guardians**
   If you are the last living parent and you die leaving children under age 18, a guardian will be appointed by the court unless you have one specified in your will. If unmarried with children, you might not even get guardianship of your own children if one of you dies. You should appoint each other as guardians in your wills to overcome this problem.

5. **Trust the trustees**
   If you are setting up a trust in your will or if your beneficiaries could be aged under 18 when you die, you will

need to appoint trustees to manage things until it passes to the beneficiaries. They must have a good grasp of financial matters – and be young enough not to die before you do.

6. Make specific legacies
   If you want to pass down family heirlooms or sentimental items leave them as a specific legacy to a named beneficiary.

7. Make sure you leave a residual legacy
   The 'residue' is what is left over in your estate after you have made any specific legacies. You must specify who this goes to as, if you fail to do so, you will create a partial intestacy in your will.

8. Save tax with trust
   Inheritance Tax is becoming a burden for many families these days. If you are married, consider a discretionary trust in your wills, which could save your children thousands in IHT. For many the new 2007 rules have eased this by doubling up on the nil rate band.

9. Sign your will
   Sign it in front of two independent witnesses or it will not be valid. A witness cannot be anyone mentioned in the will or anyone married to anyone mentioned in the will.

10. Store it safely
    Once signed and witnessed, store it safely, but don't hide it. Tell your executors where it is – it's no good to anyone if it can't be found when you've gone.

Proof after death

For IHT, regular gifts made out of your surplus income get left out of your estate when calculating any tax due after your death. OK, but how easy will it be for your executors to prove this to the Taxman?

Gifts that fall within the exemption must not affect your standard of living and should be part of a regular pattern of spending. This is your income after deducting tax, normal living expenses and outgoings. There is no financial ceiling to limit the amount you could give away. (Such gifts out of surplus income are in addition to the annual exempt amount of £3,000.)

You are entitled to make gifts up to a level of your net surplus. If this was, for example, £10,000 a year, this would reduce the eventual IHT bill by £4,000 a year. You don't even have to wait seven years for the exemption to apply. The overriding consideration is that the gifts become part of your normal expenditure without having an effect on your standard of living.

Records are the key if you decide to go down this route. Make a record of your income and outgoings in sufficient detail to evidence the surplus income. Prepare a schedule of gifts made on an annual basis, detailing dates, amounts and beneficiaries. Doing this each year establishes the regularity of the gifts. The regular gifts don't have to be to the same person or group of people. Retain supporting evidence of your income, e.g. copies of tax returns, income certificates and bank statements.

TOP TIP

Keep your records with your will and update them annually – perhaps a good time to do so is when you complete your tax return. There is no need to tell the Taxman now about what you've done. It'll be up to your executors to submit the details when dealing with your estate. They have a duty not to act negligently, which is what they would be doing if they just treated all your gifts as out of surplus income without proof.

Other escape routes

There are a number of exemptions which allow you to pass on amounts (during your lifetime or in your will) without IHT falling due, but whatever you do, keep the evidence in a safe and accessible place, e.g. copies of letters, bank statements, copies of cheques, and copy them to your solicitor or accountant to be doubly safe.

Use it or lose it

You can give away £3,000 every tax year free of IHT. You carry forward all or part of the unused £3,000 exemption to the next year but no further. This means you could give away up to £6,000 in any one year if you hadn't used any of your exemption the year before.

Give to save

Most gifts or transfers made more than seven years before your death are exempt, as are certain other gifts.

Give away to the following at any time or in your will to escape IHT:

- Your spouse or civil partner, even if you're legally separated (but not if you've divorced or the civil partnership has dissolved) as long as you both have a permanent home in the UK.

- UK charities.

- Some national institutions, including national museums, universities and the National Trust.

- UK political parties.

- But watch out – gifts to your unmarried partner, or a partner with whom you've not formed a civil partnership, aren't exempt.

Boost the wedding list

Wedding or civil partnership ceremony gifts (to either of the couple) are exempt from Inheritance Tax up to certain amounts:

- Parents can each give £5,000.

- Grandparents and other relatives can each give £2,500.

- Anyone else can give £1,000.

But watch the timing – to qualify you have to make the gift on or shortly before the date of the wedding or civil partnership ceremony. Make it too soon and if the couple call off the ceremony you'll be caught!

Small is beautiful

You can make small annual gifts, up to the value of £250, to as many people as you like without them being liable for IHT. But you can't give a larger sum, e.g. £500, and claim exemption for the first £250. Also you can't use this exemption with any other exemption when giving to the same person. In other words, you can't combine a 'small gifts exemption' with a 'wedding exemption' and give one of your children £5,250 when they tie the knot.

Having a 'Pet'

If you, as an individual, make a gift to another individual and it isn't covered by one of the above exemptions, it is known as a 'potentially exempt transfer' (PET). A PET is only free of IHT if you live for seven years after you make the gift. PETs must be outright gifts – with no strings attached. Fail to cut the strings by say, gifting a house but remaining there rent free, will mean it still counts as part of your estate no matter how long you live. There are other rules on how much tapered tax your beneficiaries pay if you die within seven years (see HMRC website).

The "dead" line

IHT is generally payable within six months from the end of the month of death – miss the deadline and interest will be added to your bill. On assets such as land and buildings a deferred and instalment plan can be arranged over 10 years.

Passing the house down

Watch out for pitfalls involved in giving your home away to your kids during your lifetime – it can have a way of falling down around you ears!

- If you stay put, without paying a full market rent, it's not an 'outright gift' but a 'gift with reservation' so it's still treated as part of your estate, and so liable for IHT.

- Any rent you pay to your children will be subject to tax in their hands.

- Under the pre-owned assets IT regime, you could be caught for tax if you give cash to the kids to buy a bigger house for you all to live in. Take advice and fund a large extension instead for their current house and move into that as a tax efficient annexe.

- Children assuming legal ownership of your home could later divorce or face bankruptcy. This could see your home being sold to fund a settlement.

- Unless the children occupy the house as their main residence – they will have to pay CGT on any increase in its value when it is sold.

- An alternative would be to sell outright and move to a smaller and cheaper property. Passing down excess cash to the kids instead may escape IHT under the PET rules – provided that you survive seven years.

- Equity Release schemes as a method of using the value of your house to raise money, carry many risks and I cannot over emphasise the need for proper advice here.

Vary the will

Within two years of a death, the family can agree to draw up a deed of variation as an IHT planning tool. This is a legal way to alter someone's will after their death, provided all the beneficiaries involved agree. If it is properly executed, and the Revenue is notified within six months, the tax consequences for IHT and for CGT are as if the original will had always had the wording given it by the deed of variation.

This can be an extremely valuable IHT planning tool, as often family members only discover that they have a problem after the death, when their adviser calculates the IHT bill (!) but it's no excuse for not planning at a much earlier stage!

Summary

To reduce the IHT, say 'I will' to the following:

1. Asset transfers between spouses and civil partners.
2. The first £3,000 of lifetime transfers in any tax year plus any unused balance from previous year.
3. Gifts of up to £250 p.a. to any number of persons.
4. Gifts in consideration of marriage or civil partnership: up to £5,000 by a parent, up to £2,500 by a grandparent, or up to £1,000 by any other person.
5. Gifts made out of income forming part of normal expenditure, which does not reduce your standard of living.
6. Gifts to charities.
7. Gifts to political parties.

" The best measure of a man's honesty isn't his Income Tax return. It's the zero adjust on his bathroom scale. "

Arthur C. Clarke

chapter 4
Top records tips

Despite moving towards a 'paperless' society, HMRC love you to keep records, especially if you are in business, and this can lead to boxes of books adding to your loft insulation.

So what should you keep?

Basically, anything you use to complete your tax return and accounts and if you have a capital gain you may need to refer to some pretty old acquisition records as well.

You can keep your records on a computer but if any tax has been deducted from the income you will also need to keep the original hard copy certificates. To avoid potential fines you will have to hang on to them for some years too!

It's worth remembering that in the case of a Revenue investigation or enquiry, HMRC's powers allow them the same access to your records held on a computer as would be allowed if they were paper documents.

HMRC's own internal IT experts, armed with specialist software, can interrogate your accounting systems to expose items booked through the business and what's really behind the façade of those beautifully bound accounts. Keep those books safe, as you are expected to inform HMRC immediately if any are permanently lost or destroyed – putting you straight in the spotlight.

Get organised

For every Tax Year:

1. Use a folder to keep all your tax return information together.

2. Throughout the tax year put all tax information into the folder.

3. File documents in an orderly fashion, in both date order and category, e.g. dividend vouchers, interest certificates, etc.

4. Prepare a schedule for each of the main categories in your tax folder, such as your dividend income, share acquisitions and disposals, bank interest.

5. Place a photocopy of last year's return in the wallet for comparison.

6. Mark your diary or calendar on 1st July – "Do my tax return".

7. If you use an accountant, prepare a personal information schedule for him including full name, address, email, home, work, mobile and fax numbers, NI number, tax reference, date of birth, sex, and same information for spouse.

8. Additional useful information is marital status, residence status, for children (up to 19), their full names and dates of birth, and if widowed the date of spouse's death.

9. Attach a copy of death certificate.

10. Keep evidence of gifts made during the year.

11. Keep proof of windfalls, gambling wins, legacies and gifts.

All the Ps

If you are an employee you will need the following for your annual tax return:

- P60 (end of year statement of pay and tax deducted).
- P45 if you have changed your job in the tax year.
- P160 if you retire and go on to receive a work-related pension.
- Particulars of work-related income, i.e. tips, not included on form P60.
- P9D or P11D re any benefits in kind and expenses payments received.
- Personally paid work-related subscriptions.
- P2 coding notice.

Pensioners' paperwork

Keep safe:

- Paperwork you receive showing the amount of state benefits/pension.
- P60 for each work-related pension.
- Paperwork re retirement annuities from a pre-July 1988 pension policy.
- Your coding notice.

Important evidence

If you receive income from UK investments such as a bank, building societies or dividend income or any income from trusts, ensure you have:

- Bank or building society passbooks, statements and certificates.
- Statements or certificates in connection with other investments.
- UK company dividend vouchers including those where shares are received instead of cash, and any tax vouchers in respect of holdings of unit trusts.
- Insurance company paperwork re gains on a life insurance policy.
- UK trust income certificates from the trustees.
- Any other useful information connected to your investments or savings.

Safe not sorry

Keep all bank statements neatly filed for six years in case the taxman calls for them as to obtain duplicates will cost you dearly in time as well as money. Banks charge "per statement" and can also take many weeks to produce them.

Gains and losses

If you have a capital gain or capital loss it is worth keeping a separate folder re purchases and sales. Keep all contract notes, completion statements, etc. This will include property (apart from your own home), shares or other assets you give away or sell. Keep any valuations of the assets too if carried out.

- If you have a property and carry out improvements, keep the expenditure invoices plus estate agent's fees, stamp duty and legal bills.
- If you receive an asset as a gift or an inheritance, keep the evidence, like solicitor's letters or accounts.
- Retain copies of bank statements and chequebook stubs in connection with the sale or improvement of your assets.
- If you use your own home for business or you let out part of it, maintain full records of dates and rooms used, and take photos too.

No record, no claim

To claim any reliefs or deductions, you must retain:

- Details of payments made under Gift Aid.
- Certificates of pension payments made.
- Court orders in connection with maintenance payments paid by those born before 6 April 1935.
- Lender's interest paid certificates.

Business books

If you trade as a self-employed sole trader or partnership you need a system for keeping your records and it is very important you keep your personal records separate from those for your business, including keeping business and private cash separate.

The Revenue says that they will normally expect you to:

- Record all sales and other business receipts as they come in.
- Keep back-up records, e.g. copy invoices, till rolls, cheque stubs, bank statements, and paying-in slips.
- Record all purchases and other expenses as they arise and ensure that you retain invoices.
- Keep a record of all purchases and sales of assets used in your business.
- Record all amounts taken out of the business bank account, or in cash, for your own personal use.
- Record all amounts paid into the business from personal funds or assets introduced.

Which accounting books you need to keep depends mainly on the size of your business but you should at the very least have a cash book. This would include payments to and from your bank, cash income and payments and any amounts you take out of the business. You may also want to keep a separate petty cash book for your day to day small cash transactions.

Other evidence to substantiate your business transactions might include:

- If you use your own home for your business, household bills to allocate running costs between private and business use.
- If you do not have a separate business and private bank account, keep an accurate record of which expenses are business and which are private.
- Wages records, for employees or subcontractors, to support all payments made.
- Using a car or van for the business means keeping a log of business mileage and details of both running costs and fuel.

Cover your back

- Set aside time each week to file your business records efficiently.
- Lose a receipt and you lose the chance to claim.
- Order duplicate bank statements that have gone missing.
- Never amend your books with Tipp-Ex or write in pencil and rub out. You may think it makes a neat job, the taxman will think it covers up the true picture.
- Make sure invoice numbers run consecutively; gaps or cancelled invoices will need an explanation, so write it down as it happens.
- Never deliberately destroy records you know you need, it can lead to serious consequences.
- Note down incidents like thefts or losses of stock or money or even bad weather, as they happen if they affect trade.
- There's a possible £3,000 fine for failing to keep the required records. It's seldom applied, but don't let your case be the first.

Taxing forms

The hard work in completing your tax return is not filling in the boxes, but gathering together the records and information you need. Don't leave it too late for the filing deadline.

You may need:

- Extra tax return pages.
- Certificates of Bank Interest received.
- Certificates of Loan Interest paid.
- Duplicate Bank Statements.
- Share dividend vouchers.
- P60.
- P11D.
- Pension Statements.

Some things can take up to six weeks to arrive and that could be too late.

Bean counters briefing

Here are some useful terms for book-keeping beginners:

1. **Nominal account**

   Each of the items that make up the balance sheet is a nominal account. Accountants have a significant number of nominal accounts for all fixed assets and different types of income and expenditure.

2. **Nominal ledger**

   All the nominal accounts make up the nominal ledger. Nowadays it is typically part of a computer programme.

3. **Trial balance**

   The trial balance (or 'TB') is just a listing of all the nominal accounts showing the balance in each, like a very detailed balance sheet.

4. **Purchase ledger**

   Most businesses have scores of suppliers. It is very important to keep detailed records of all transactions with suppliers, so a separate ledger is maintained for this purpose. Purchase ledgers are linked to the nominal ledger so that whenever a change is made to the purchase ledger, the relevant accounts in the nominal ledger (e.g. trade creditors, cash) are automatically updated.

5. **Sales ledger**

   The sales ledger is the equivalent of the purchase ledger for customer records.

6. **Posting**

   'Posting' a transaction means entering it into the relevant ledgers.

7. **Audit trail**

   A listing kept by all accounting systems of every transaction posted on to the system.

8. **Journal entry**

   A journal entry is an adjustment made to the nominal ledger (i.e. to two or more nominal accounts), often at the year-end.

Time flies

On a monthly basis, as you receive them, annotate your bank statements with details of the source of any unusual or private deposits to your bank accounts. I will guarantee that you will fail to recall easily that gift from granny, lottery windfall or insurance payout when years later the taxman queries it. Keep the evidence too to ensure he keeps his hands off your money.

Take care

The Revenue takes a tough line on carelessness and non-compliance. Taxpayers face penalties or even prosecution if they are negligent or fraudulent, therefore complete and accurate records can be your saviour.

So to summarise:

1. Before you start your return, make sure the Revenue has sent you everything you need. The form has several sections and they will only send those that it thinks apply to you. Check if you need extra pages to give details of other sources of income.

2. Keep accurate records. If you face a Revenue enquiry you will have to produce evidence that your tax return is correct.

3. Dig out everything you need. If you're self-employed you will need details of your earnings and expenses. You will also need other sources of information such as bank statements and share dividend statements.

4. Don't throw away your records. Taxpayers must keep records for at least a year after filing. Self-employed or business owners must keep records for six years.

5. Don't leave things until the last minute. Once you have gathered all the necessary paperwork, put aside a large part of the day to go through the forms. The biggest mistake people make is forgetting to sign the form before sending it off. It will bounce back and give HMRC the chance for a second look.

6. If your affairs are complicated, seek advice from either a tax specialist or the Revenue's own help line.

7. As well as paying tax you owe for the last tax year, you might also need to make a payment on account for the current tax year. This is calculated on the basis of your previous year's earnings. In most cases you work this out by halving your liability for the last tax year. You pay half of what you owe on account in January and half in July.

   Payments on account can be reduced if you have reasonable grounds to expect your tax to be lower than that of the previous year. Keep cash flow forecasts and put aside the tax each month to avoid a big lump sum shock.

"I have trouble
    reconciling my net
income with my
        gross habits."

Errol Flynn

chapter 5
Surviving an investigation

You are a million times more likely to be the subject of a tax investigation than seeing your lottery numbers come up on a Saturday night.

HMRC can and do select some tax returns for an in-depth enquiry entirely at random, but these are few and far between. The vast majority of investigations are mounted following what the Revenue call their "risk assessment". Risk being the likelihood that tax is being lost to the Treasury. In the main, the group pond from which they fish is that containing the self-employed and companies.

Generally around 3% of sole trader and partnership tax returns are picked up for a full investigation every year with a lesser percentage for companies.

Nowadays the taxman has dropped the term "investigation" in favour of the less confrontational "enquiry" – but the process remains the same and the basics have not changed much over the years. In the eyes of poor businessmen and women, being investigated by the Revenue remains one of their greatest worries. Ignorance of tax law has never been accepted as an excuse for getting it wrong – so for you, the taxpayer, knowledge is power. The following tips and tools should help you take steps to avoid selection for investigation or at least minimise the damage as 'it could be you'.

Deal or no deal

In virtually all in-depth investigations by HMRC, negotiation ("horse-trading" or "doing a deal") has been the driving force behind finally agreed settlement figures. It's what's kept me in a job — brokering deals which keep the client happy, as well as solvent, and satisfy the Taxman that the stinging "slap on the wrist" has been administered. Aggressive moves are afoot within HMRC to do away with "all-inclusive package deals" in favour of taking taxpayers on expensive, litigious "long-haul" journeys. For me it's business as usual.

In the dark

In law the taxman has a massive opportunity in terms of time and scope in which to gather information on you, to check out your business premises and private home, lifestyle and cars. Following submission of your return, he has a window of a year in order to launch an enquiry into your affairs.

You may well receive a calculation setting out the tax due — but this does not mean that they agree this. They operate on a "Process Now, Check Later" basis, so don't hold your breath, as you have a long wait until you can be certain that window of opportunity has closed.

Showing interest in your interest

Work on the assumption that HMRC are aware of all bank and building society interest you receive — including that from children's and offshore accounts. Take care not to omit any bank account from your tax return — and include only your share of accounts held jointly.

An omitted bank account is a sure-fire way of triggering an enquiry as is any unexplained increase or decrease in the level of interest. Why?

Their sinister suspicion – you have sold an asset or property and failed to declare it, or alternatively acquired one.

Your innocent explanation – you have received a legacy or paid for your daughter's very expensive wedding!

You may wonder why he is so keen on checking your bank interest when it has already suffered tax of 20%; well in truth it's the source of the underlying capital that he's interested in and the interest received just gives him the clue and the foot in the door.

The brown envelope

Inside is what they call the "opening letter" telling you that HMRC are making enquiries into you tax return.

Anxious, confused, upset and angry you will be – nonchalant and in denial you must not be. Stacking brown envelopes behind the clock on the mantelpiece may be OK for some – but they are likely to see the clock disappear into the back of the bailiff's van in very short order.

- Read the letter and the Code of Practice (COP) fully and check the date to ensure it's within the legal timeframe.
- Take advice from your accountant or specialist tax adviser immediately.
- Don't delay – it can cost you money.
- Respond in writing to every single query relating to your business, factually and concisely.

- Provide access to the business records (and they are entitled to them in electronic format if held).

- Do not provide records outside of the accounts year in question.

- Do not provide any private/personal records or private bank statements.

TOP TIP

Don't panic, but do be worried. Worry can be beneficial if channelled into positive action. A certain amount of fear of the unknown can enable you to focus better on the job in hand.

Economical with the response

Bank accounts or credit cards used in any way for business purposes are linked to the business and are fair game for HMRC.

- Do not destroy any business records.

- Keep it to yourself – canvassing opinion and gossip will elicit a variety of opinions, invariably wrong. The 'man in the pub' always knows everything but he will not be the one representing you in front of the taxman.

- Explain anything of major importance having an affect on the return – say a serious illness affecting profits.

- Don't assume the enquiry will go away if you ignore it – it won't.

- Copy all letters received and documents sent to HMRC and record the date posted.

- Keep everything in a separate file in chronological order.

- Make a note of all telephone conversations with the Revenue – including date, time, and name of the person you spoke to; Revenue opinions differ depending upon who you are speaking to! And remember "if it's not written down it didn't happen!".

- Include your own reference number on the top of all letters and documents sent to the Revenue. They have a habit of losing things – even their own files and discs occasionally!

- Always ask for their reply by a set date – allowing them no more than 30 days to reply and return your records.

- Don't put your negative feelings about the enquiry or the Inspector in writing. Sarcasm is the lowest form of wit and he may not have a good sense of humour anyway! Don't be tempted to telephone him – abuse goes down like a lead balloon and will jeopardise your case, and they can spot "he who protesteth too much" a mile off.

- Don't expect a prompt reply to your letters. Typically letters notifying the next stage take about a month. Any longer make a note of it – it will be useful later in mitigating any penalty charges.

- When sending them your business records don't suffer heavy postage costs. Take them to you nearest tax office and ask them to organise collection from there. Alternatively, make the taxman examine them at your accountant's premises.

Serious and even more serious

There are basically two different types of full enquiry:

- Local tax office enquiries.
- Cases of suspected serious fraud, dealt with by Civil Investigation of Fraud (CIF) teams or the Special Civil Investigation (SCI) officers, the latter taking on the higher monetary value cases.

You will be in no doubt from the first letter which one relates to you – from the accompanying Code of Practice (COP). Both encourage your voluntary co-operation.

The Codes of Practice (COP) setting out the two very different practices are available on HMRC's website. Check them out by typing in "COP11" and "COP 9".

There are common objectives running through both types of enquiry and prosecution can be avoided in both, provided you do not make deliberately false statements. However in the CIF/SCI cases the stakes are higher in terms of the likely tax yield, stress levels, and professional fees. Specialist tax advice is not just recommended but essential.

At the outset the inspector will not tell you the reason for his enquiry. A good tax specialist will usually be able to read between the lines and spot the reason from the initial letter, or perhaps you personally will have a good idea!

If not, the reason will normally become clear once the inspector has examined your records and called for an interview.

A local tax office enquiry is likely to last around 6-18 months, with the more serious CIF/SCI cases extending over 1-2 years. A large chunk of your life and finances are at stake and you will need the support of family and professionals.

On the ropes

In local district enquiries (not including a suspicion of fraud), it has long been common practice for Inspectors to seek at least one meeting with the taxpayer and his agent during the course of an investigation, normally after he has rummaged through your books and bank accounts. The spectre of a face to face confrontation with the taxman often strikes a chill of fear through the heart of even the most hard-nosed businessman.

HMRC's own internal instructions tell the Inspector not to seek a meeting as a matter of routine, and you the taxpayer cannot be compelled by law to attend. Yes, you do not have to go—it's entirely up to you—but this is the Revenue's big secret in their attempt to find out about your lifestyle "straight from the horse's mouth".

Confusing reasons with excuses

1. The excuse
   We would like to meet with you, preferably at your business premises, in order to gain a better understanding of your business and how it's operated.

2. The reason
   Really they want to size you up, go through your records with a fine toothcomb and discuss your finances, including your private affairs, in more detail than your own spouse

would dare! They want you to talk and when you're nervous you will – so take a spade with you because you will be digging yourself a great big hole.

3. **The defence**

    The taxman's only job is to check that the figures included on your tax return are complete and correct. It is none of their business to understand yours!

    He has no right of access (under his ordinary legal powers) to your business premises or home. He can enter only at your invitation – and it's unlikely that a gold embossed one would be winging its way to him any time soon.

    Therefore, you can "RSVP" to him, apologising for your unavailability at any time and there's nothing in law he can do to insist on your attendance. He will however be sorely disappointed. Nothing excites them more than luring an unsuspecting taxpayer into their lair – especially one who's totally unprepared.

Do I stay or do I go?

Ask yourself the question:

"Who is gaining the most from the meeting?" Nine times out of ten it won't be you! If you are in the range of 'shy and nervous' to 'downright paranoid or aggressive' then DON'T GO. It's within your rights to conduct the Q and A back and forth by correspondence – but lately the Revenue are wising up to the growing reluctance to meet with them and the length of their letters are depleting the average rain forest! And you'll see that their letters are now sent out on flimsy grey recycled paper – I rest my case.

Correspondence can and does drag on and is an unlikely method of cutting the time or professional costs of the enquiry – even if it does save your face.

The better options are:

A. Instruct a tax investigation specialist, who will take you through a dummy interview briefing you fully on what to expect and then attend with you – thus preventing the Inspector from overstepping the mark.

B. After discussions, instruct the tax specialist to go to the meeting for you. It will be a shorter more focused meeting and he or she will field the questions appropriately and deal with the replies for you.

C. Buy this book and read on – thus saving you a lot of money on A and B and hopefully saving you tax by doing it yourself – properly prepared!

So, for the sake of those choosing route C, who have decided a face to face meeting will not be to their disadvantage – here we go with the guidance, for a D.I.Y job. For the rest of you it will serve to tell you exactly what to expect.

Location, location, location

The choice is yours:

Business premises or your home will be strongly suggested and I say no, just as strongly, to both.

If you have neutral territory available, this would provide the most relaxed environment for you. The other side are playing away from home and will have to do all the travelling and bag carrying and will be constantly aware of the full time whistle.

Just don't offer them a drink at half time and you can always hope that the disadvantage makes them score an own goal!

Whenever a meeting takes place away from his home ground the Inspector will bring along a supporter – usually to take notes, sometimes a trainee. But beware, occasionally an officer from a Civil Investigation of Fraud team or a qualified Revenue Accountant will be playing on his side – especially if potentially there is a lot at stake or complicated technical issues are involved.

The vast majority of tax inspectors are not accountants but they will put themselves across to an unsuspecting victim as an expert – often they are no more expert than you are. Agree the venue in advance in writing, and ask who is attending and what position they are playing in the game, before kick off. (It goes without saying that if a CIF officer is involved, drop the D.I.Y. route.)

Good timing

- Go for a 2pm appointment to help limit the duration – most Revenue employees like to be on their way home soon after 4pm.

- Time really does fly in meetings with HMRC – when you ramble on and are given the silent treatment to digress to your heart's content.

- Retain the focus and control by agreeing a time limit on it to, say, 2 hours max.

- Time's money – for you, and your accountant. Cut the costs by holding a short, sharp meeting.

- Accept that stress happens – but keep the lid on it by being cool, calm and collected with an agreed end time as your goal. Place your watch on the table and structure your answers within that time frame. The end will come and you will have got your points across, but don't be afraid to take a break at anytime if you need it – or take a friend with you for moral support.

Hidden agenda

Get an agenda from the Inspector up front; he has to give it to you. The downside is, it will be very general and reveal no actual concerns and few specific questions. "Hardly worth the recycled paper it's written on" comes to mind – as they hope that one question will lead to another.

But make him stick to it – he'll hate it. Each partner or spouse has a right to privacy – you do not have to discuss your affairs in front of each other – so either waive your confidentiality or ask for two separate agendas and meetings.

HMRC's aim is for Inspectors to move towards an arena of "openness and early dialogue" but this may not always be the taxpayer's preferred option! More detailed agendas may soon be the order of the day offering user friendly introductions, explanations of procedures, opportunities for quicker taxpayer disclosures, flexibility and agreed time frames. For now it may still be a case of the blind leading those who will not see!

The meeting

Questions will always relate to a trading period possibly going back 3 years. This is his interview 'brief', though unfortunately, it won't be!

1. The Inspector's preamble about his legal obligations to be satisfied about the accuracy of your return and your human rights. He will not tell you why you have been selected for investigation (though over the next couple of hours it might become abundantly clear).

2. He'll ask you if you are happy that your return is correct and complete and if you have anything to disclose at this early stage.

3. Questions on your business — what you do and how you do it.

- History.
- Outlets.
- Employees.
- Your role.
- Hours.

4. Specific Areas:

- Products/Services.
- Pricing Policy.
- Competition and suppliers.
- Customer base.
- Cash/Cheques/Credit Card percentages.
- Incidental/Ancillary income.
- Wastage.
- Thefts.
- Profit fluctuations.

5. The records – he will only review the books for one year, the year of enquiry. This is the big one. Any errors or omissions here mean potentially incorrect accounts/returns and therefore possible losses of tax going back many years.

He'll want to know about:

- The chain of events – what records are kept, who keeps them, and when.
- What are the 'prime' records – till rolls, calendars, work diaries, job sheets, and time sheets?
- A review of all sales and purchase invoices.
- Banking practices.
- Wages and Drawings procedures.
- Cash control.
- Float levels.
- Petty cash.
- Minimum and maximum cash held.

Once he's "broken the records" – he holds all the cards to put you under serious financial pressure.

6. Private usage of your car, phone or goods from stock.

7. Getting personal.
   Where the records review throws up concerns (sales or drawings look too low, expenses too high) he'll be into you in some depth regarding your 'private side' of life.

First he closes the 'loopholes' by establishing receipt of any tax free 'windfalls', e.g. legacies, pools/lottery wins, cash gifts, sales of chattels, etc.

You will then be expected to put a price on family weekly, monthly or annual spending. OK, what man would know this, and what woman would genuinely be able to remember what she spent last month, let alone last year! Don't be pressured – if in doubt say nowt!

The black, the white and the grey

Hold your hands up to any proven 'black marks' against you – the obvious existence of property or bank accounts.

Maximise where you have been 'whiter then white' – under claiming allowable business expenditure, no inadequacy in your ability to fund personal spending.

Negotiate on the grey areas – defend yourself on levels of cash possibly omitted from the books, the correct uplifted gross profit rate which applies, or how much you and the family spend.

Any additional profit you agree for the enquiry year will then be used to calculate similar uplifts for the earlier years—often using a 'broad brush'—so keep it down for the target year and beat them down for the earlier ones.

In law they can go back up to 20 years – but in local district enquiries the average is to collect "back tax" for six.

Top meeting tips

- You can only make one first impression – be polite, never rude.
- Don't arrive late.
- Never guess – offer to provide an account later.
- Stick to the year in question – not what has gone on since then.
- Don't feel intimidated – only you know the answers so ask him to explain if you don't understand.
- Be honest and answer only what you are asked.
- Meetings are never taped.
- Make notes of your own if you wish. Ask questions, it may be the only chance you get.
- Know your rights – do you need professional advice?
- Don't panic and keep calm.
- Eat and drink something before you go, but never alcohol!
- Put plenty of money in the meter/car park.
- Protect your reputation by keeping it to yourself when you leave the meeting.
- It can be a hugely humbling and shameful experience but remember "No-one ever died of embarrassment".
- Never lie.
- Never lie.
- Oh yes, and finally... NEVER LIE!

What not to say…

"I don't smoke, drink or go out socially"
They've heard it hundreds of times before and the nicotine stains or beer belly are a dead give away!

"I've nothing to hide"
Their eyes will glaze over at this, as it seldom turns out to be true, however optimistically you put it across.

"My accountant told me I could claim it"
It may be true but the responsibility rests with you. Sadly, you cannot hide behind your accountant if he's made a mistake – you are liable for the consequences. Ignorance is not a valid excuse.

"I don't need cash"
Try doing without it! Or see how long you can really hang on to that £10 from the cash machine. You may be surprised.

"I have no hobbies or interests"
OK, if you are sure that the subscription to the golf club won't show in your cheque stubs or the direct debit for the gym won't jump out at them, go ahead.

"I hardly ever use the car privately"
They will check out annual mileage travelled from your MOT certificates etc.

"But none of my mates give an invoice for all jobs"
Whoops – names and addresses please! The taxman loves to compile a dossier of defaulters with your help. It could be how your enquiry arose!

The aftermath

After the meeting the Inspector will send you a copy of his notes of it – and ask you to sign them.

- They are comprehensive but not verbatim.
- No it wasn't taped!
- They may appear biased.
- Don't be afraid to challenge any points.
- Record your version and put it to him for amendment.
- Never sign the notes – it's difficult to retract later.
- What you said will be 'tested' – he will try to find discrepancies between what you said and what the paper records show.

More questions could follow or a proposal for settling the enquiry – more than likely involving additional tax.

Interest and penalties

Interest is charged on all tax paid late – end of story. It cannot be avoided. They want their interest on the 'free loan' you've had from the Treasury in respect of the tax you've hung on to.

They will want a penalty too and can get it as you will have at least failed to check reasonably carefully that your return, accounts or records were correct. It does not have to be a fraudulent act to trigger the penalty charge.

Briefly here's how it's calculated:

The penalty is based on the amount of tax that was unpaid. If you have underpaid £6,000 tax, the maximum penalty for this would be £6,000. In practice, the penalty is always reduced from this maximum by taking the following three factors into consideration:

- Disclosure
  The maximum reduction in the penalty is up to 20% for "disclosure". "Disclosure" means admitting any mistakes you have made or profits you have understated, as soon as the Inland Revenue challenges you. (There's an extra 10% for those who go to the Revenue voluntarily and hold their hands up to what has gone wrong.)

- Cooperation
  Cooperation is the next factor that should always get you a reduction of the full 40%. This is why it's important not to ignore any letters or requests from the Inspector, and deal with him promptly and politely; but balance this with a firm stance, within your rights and do not merely roll over in response to his veiled threats or unreasonable requests.

- Seriousness
  Finally the penalty can be reduced by up to 40% depending on the seriousness of the tax irregularities. This discount varies greatly in all cases when looking at the level of tax owed and how heinous the reason behind it. Your actions will fall somewhere between premeditated and well-organised fraud, and something a great deal less serious.

Looking back you will see that the maximum discounts could come to 110% – they never do!

This relies on the extra 10% for full and complete voluntary disclosure but whatever the outcome the taxman will never pay you money back!

An average penalty level would be calculated as:

	Discount	Charge
Disclosure	10%	10%
Co-operation	40%	NIL
Seriousness	20%	20%
	=70%	=30%

A done deal

First a reminder: Inspectors should work under the premise of only being there to collect the right amount of tax and no more. The reminder is for them not you! Let's take it that both sides have now agreed – with a good deal of compromise by both parties. You may not be happy to pay up but you are now willing and a lot wiser.

The paperwork involved is:

1. Contract settlement

   If you agree to make an offer, you have to sign a formal letter offering to pay the agreed sum within a stated period. If HMRC are happy with it, they will then issue a letter of acceptance, forming a contract legally binding both sides by its terms.

2. Certificate of full disclosure

   As the previous tax return declarations you signed have been found seriously lacking, this form confirms that you have now made a complete disclosure to them of all income and assets between certain dates. Read the accompanying notes (94E) carefully as false statements can and do lead to prosecution.

If in doubt call the Inspector before signing your life away.

3. Statement of assets and liabilities
   Commonly requested at the beginning and end of an
   enquiry. You will be asked to supply details of your personal
   assets, liabilities and business interests. It carries the same
   health warning as 2.

You do not have to use the form provided and can instead use
your own format but it must be signed. It covers your worldwide
assets and your minor children's too. It's a useful form to prove
that you lack the means to pay over a large tax settlement too,
in order to ask for a reduction.

BENs and TIPs

Business Economic Notes (BENs) give background information
into certain trades and were originally only intended for the
investigating officer's eyes. Now they're available for you all
to see, and are very useful in giving you an insight into how
the taxman thinks your business operates and how much it
makes! Forewarned is forearmed, so give them a glance on
HMRC's website.

The downside is of course, that in possession of a whole
armoury of statistics with which to attack you, the Taxman in
his mind becomes a "jack of all trades". So never lose sight of
the fact that no one knows your business better than you and
that in reality, he is "master of none".

	Business Economic Notes (BENs)
No.	Trade
26	Confectioners, Tobacconists and Newsagents
25	Taxicabs and Private Hire Vehicles
24	Independent Fishmongers
23	Driving Instructors
22	Dispensing Chemists
21	Residential Rest and Nursing Homes
20	Insurance Brokers and Agents
19	Farming – Stock Valuation for Income Tax Purposes
18	Catering – Fast Foods, Cafes and Snack Bars
17	Catering – Restaurants
16	Catering – General
15	Veterinary Surgeons
14	The Pet Industry
13	Fish and Chip Shops
12	Antique and Fine Art Dealers
11	Electrical Retailers
10	Jewellery Trade
9	Licensed Victuallers
8	Florists
7	Dentists
6	Funeral Directors
5	Waste Materials Reclamation and Disposal
4	Hairdressers
3	Lodging Industry
2	Road Haulage
1	Travel Agents

Tactical and Information Packages (TIPs) were issued in 2007 giving tactical information to inspectors to help them identify risk areas within your business.

TIPs Subject Areas
Bookmakers
Confectioners, Tobacconists and Newsagents
Construction Industry
Estate Agents
Field Sports
Franchises
Licensed Traders
Mortgage Brokers
Waste Disposal and Landfill Sites

Merging forces against fraud

The Inland Revenue merged with HM Customs and Excise in April 2005 – becoming HM Revenue and Customs, strengthening and extending their powers to fight tax evasion.

You'll know if you're under the scrutiny of a Civil Investigation of Fraud (CIF) team because you will have received not only a letter but their Code of Practice 9 setting out their stall. Yes, they want your co-operation and involvement, but their enquiry will go on regardless in their relentless crusade to uncover the full facts and collect any tax due from you. So be advised and go with the flow. Attend meetings and keep up the momentum for a quicker and less stressful result.

Provided you are open and honest from day one, the offer of COP 9 procedures will ensure you do not find yourself on the wrong end of a Revenue criminal prosecution. It may well seriously affect your sleep pattern and pocket, but you will retain your liberty, business, and family life.

Make a materially false statement or provide materially false documents with the intention to deceive and you open the door for them to consider dropping the niceties and pursuing a criminal investigation into that conduct.

TOP TIP

In CIF Investigations never adopt the ostrich position – you'll only end up with sand up the nostrils and your backside in a very weak and vulnerable position of exposure!

Prosecutions

Criminal Investigation will be reserved for cases where they need to send out a strong deterrent message or where the conduct involved is such that only a criminal route is appropriate.

HMRC reserve complete discretion to conduct a criminal investigation in any case and to carry out these investigations across a range of offences and in all the areas for which the Commissioners of HMRC have responsibility.

Top 10 triggers

1. Organised or systematic fraud including conspiracy.

2. Individual holding positions of trust or responsibility.

3. Materially false statements are made or materially false documents are provided in the course of a civil investigation.

4. Suspected deliberate concealment, deception, conspiracy or corruption.

5. Use of false or forged documents.

6. Importation or exportation, breaching prohibitions and restrictions.

7. Money laundering cases.

8. Perpetrator has committed previous offences or there is a repeated course of unlawful conduct or a previous civil action;

9. Theft, misuse or unlawful destruction of HMRC documents.

10. Evidence of assault on, threats to, or impersonation of HMRC officials or there is a link to suspected wider criminality, whether domestic or international, involving offences not under the administration of HMRC.

An inspector calls

Employers regularly face the prospect of a visit by HMRC to review their PAYE records and payroll procedures and this time they do have a right of access to your premises. Take all such visits very seriously, preferably with a specialist present to oversee the process.

If you find yourself in this position, the following should help you through it – but it's no substitute for the one-to-one advice of that tax buddy!

ALWAYS:

- Establish what time they will be leaving.
- Provide a room for the inspectors where they can be isolated from the company's staff. Don't make them too comfy!
- Show them the toilet facilities – escort them if necessary.
- Remove any notices etc, that may prove contentious – diaries, year planners, photos of the family yacht or plane!
- Brief employees about the visit and instruct them not to discuss any issues with the inspectors.
- Identify the senior person who will deal with the inspectors on the day and give them their extension number.
- Provide limited hospitality such as coffee/tea.
- Give every impression of being helpful and co-operative – smile!
- Answer questions of fact to which you know the answer. Do not waffle or guess!
- Provide only the records relevant to the enquiry as requested.

- Ask the inspectors to put in writing any comments, claims or computations.
- Make a record of the matters that the inspectors discuss, agree or drop.
- Send a copy of all communications to your accountant.

NEVER:

- Provide records that have little or no bearing on PAYE or Benefits.
- Allow the inspectors free access to junior staff, they can innocently land you right in it!
- Allow the inspectors free access to accounting records and documents, or let them roam around the premises at will.
- Provide lavish hospitality.
- Appear to be obstructive or difficult.
- Speculate or volunteer information.
- Agree any matters, calculations, arrears or irregularities on the day.
- Pay up on the day.
- Offer a bribe! HMRC staff cannot accept 'freebies'—not even a sack of spuds from the local farmer—the coffee is the limit.

Keeping mum

Try to keep 'mum' about what traumas are going on with your tax affairs—particularly avoid discussing it in front of your children—they seldom misquote you in public, in fact they normally repeat word for word everything you shouldn't have said! (It's our own fault – we spend the first two years of their lives encouraging them to walk and talk and the next sixteen telling them to sit down and shut up.)

Summary

As a Tax Inspector I was well aware that I suffered from the 'marmite effect' – people either liked me or hated me. Luckily those who did like me stuck with me for life!

At the end of the day, try to pay your tax with a smile! You won't get away with it though, they'll still want your money!

As with many stressful things in life, after the initial shock, a Tax Investigation should be handled calmly, professionally and with a large helping of common sense. Swot up on the Revenue's own rules and never be intimidated. Read the Code of Practice issued to you (as many Inspectors don't!) and get ahead of the game.

TILL ROLL TREAT
HMRC's expert till roll readers will spot the number of 'no sale' till openings per day to infer sales have been by-passed, so keep them low or be ready with a reason!

" The trick is to
stop thinking of
it as 'your money'. **"**

Revenue Auditor

chapter 6
Can claim/can't claim

Shelves are groaning under the weight of self-help guides for everything these days and unless your affairs are complex you don't have to pay for help with tax. As these tips show, there's a lot of free help out there or use them to help yourself! The Revenue makes mistakes too and nowadays is not afraid to admit to them. This could be your foot in the door to a claim for compensation.

Claim on the line

Claims to tax allowances can now be made by phone or online as well as in writing. You can claim retrospectively for a full six years prior to the current tax year. For loss relief you will usually only have two years – so note it on the calendar and don't lose track, as time flies by.

Watch this space however as moves are afoot within HMRC to severely limit the claims for earlier years' tax relief. If the Revenue get their way, back years claims could be restricted to only 4 years – wholly unfair when they retain the "status quo" to collect unpaid tax for up to 20 years. As we insiders know "fair" and "tax" never find their way into the same sentence!

Tax rebates

Everybody likes to get a tax rebate but how do you go about getting your hands on one?

- **When?**
  Either at the end of the tax year (April 5th) or when you have finished work and will not be working again in that financial year.

- **How much?**
  If you have earned less than your tax free annual allowance you will receive a full rebate of the tax you have paid.

- **How far back?**
  You can claim back tax for the previous six tax years.

- **Why?**
  Normally because you were on the wrong tax code, paying emergency tax, have not worked for the full year or work in the construction industry.

- **What's the emergency code?**
  The most common seen are WI, MI, BR, X, WKI, MTH1.

- **What if I have more than one job?**
  You have to declare your worldwide income to HMRC to receive a rebate.

- **Do I have to do a tax return?**
  Not necessarily, so check on this when claiming.

Miles ahead

The taxman allows you to claim tax-free mileage rates if you use your own car for business. But stick to the allowable rates which currently stand at:

40p per mile for first 10,000 miles.
25p per mile thereafter.

Your employer however may pay you less than this – so use the taxman to claim a rebate for the difference as below:

Step 1
Total business miles travelled say, 12,000

Step 2
First 10,000 business miles at 40p per mile   £ 4,000
Next 2,000 business miles at 25p per mile   £   500
Total tax free mileage entitlement   £ 4,500

Step 3
Less allowances received from employer   £ 3,000

Step 4
Excess amount on which tax relief can be claimed £ 1,500

Contact your own tax office and make your claim!

TRAIN STRIKE TRICK
No tax to pay on employer-provided hotels, car hire, etc., if you can't get in to work during industrial action. Or perhaps you prefer that duvet day instead?!

Logs and loopholes

If you drive a company car it is often the cheaper option to buy your own business fuel. Claim back the cost using HMRC's tax free "Advisory Fuel Rates for Company Cars". (See their website because rates change frequently as petrol prices fluctuate.)

A detailed log of business journeys is required including date, journey and accurate mileage and these must be checked and authorised by a third party. The taxman has been known to check distances using mileage checking computer software – so don't use 'round sums' or enhance the trips. Your ordinary commuting journey from home to normal permanent workplace does not count as a business trip and should be excluded.

Mileage log

The chart below should keep your claim in the clear.

Name			Registration No.			
Date	Start Mileage	Journey Details		End Mileage	Journey Bus/Priv	Driver Signature
		From	To			
Reviewed By				Date		
Authorised By				Date		

When is a benefit not a benefit?

When it is a car! Company cars and their fuel cause coding consternation as year on year the cost to the driver is hiked up – fuelling the go-green lobby. Tax is charged according to the CO_2 emissions and cost of the car – making expensive gas-guzzlers a tax efficient thing of the past.

Weigh up the cost of the company car versus using your own and claiming tax-free business mileage expenses. All circumstances vary but it's well worth doing the maths!

Man with van

A much cheaper alternative to the car could be the smart double cab pick up, classed as a van. Private use of this with unlimited fuel will currently cost you the tax on a flat fee of £3,500. It's worth a look – if you can park it.

Working at home

Arguments abound about whether your duties at home qualify for tax relief. Quite simply, now you need not put up that fight. You can claim a fixed £2 a week tax free to cover the extra heat and light you use. Claim in excess and you'll need to provide breakdowns and receipts.

On your bike

Tax relief can also be claimed for business travel by cycle or motor bike or receive tax free mileage rates from your employer in accordance with the approved rates shown on HMRC's website.

Tax-free PIEs

If you are sent to work away from home and stay in a hotel, when the firm pay for your accommodation and travel, this will not give rise to a tax charge on you. But you can receive PIEs tax free too. 'Personal Incidental Expenses' at £5 per night (£10 if abroad) can be paid to you tax free to cover things like your laundry, newspapers, and phone calls.

Trivial benefits

Employers can give items to employees tax free, if HMRC deem them 'trivial'.

Common allowable items are normally perishable or consumable. Here are some examples that won't touch employees' pockets!

- Workplace tea, coffee or water from a cooling dispenser, available generally to all employees.
- Small gifts, such as an arrangement of flowers, as long as this is made in recognition of a particular event (e.g. marriage or birth of a child) and is not part of any reward for services.
- Gifts, such as a turkey, an ordinary bottle of wine, or a box of chocolates at Christmas.

If the seasonal gifts extend beyond this to say, a case of wine or a hamper, then they fall into dangerous territory, to be viewed "objectively" and subject to the judgement of the local Revenue officer. One can only hope that his culinary tastes lean towards the more gourmet!

Child Trust Fund (CTF)

All children born on or after 1 September 2002, who live in the UK, are eligible for a £250 voucher to open a Child Trust Fund account. Children in lower-income families receive an additional payment direct into their CTF account of £250. The Government will make further payments into all CTF accounts at age 7.

The CTF is a long-term savings and investment account. Family, friends and the child themselves can contribute up to £1,200 a year in total. The money is available for the child only to withdraw at 18. Neither the parents nor the child will be taxed on any interest or gains made in the account.

Child Benefit

Child Benefit is a tax-free monthly payment to anyone bringing up a child. Income or savings do not affect it so most people who are bringing up a child or young person qualify for it.

Additional qualifying conditions apply once a child reaches 16. If you're entitled to Child Benefit for a child who is not your own, you may also be entitled to Guardian's Allowance for them if both of their parents have died or, in some circumstances, where only one parent has died.

Open the gate

The Saving Gateway (a cash saving scheme aimed at low earners) comes into effect in 2010, with the government matching in hard cash, money which people have saved in these accounts over 2 years.

Credit yourself

If you have a child under 16, you should submit a claim for Child Tax Credit even if your current family income means you don't qualify, particularly if your income tends to fluctuate or job may be in jeopardy. This way, if your income falls suddenly, you will be able to amend your claim and receive tax credit from the start. Claim later and it will only be backdated for 3 months.

Child care choice

The childcare voucher benefit scheme enables you to take part of your salary in childcare vouchers. It brings significant financial benefits to employees.

The amount of vouchers one person can take is currently capped at £55 per week or £243 per calendar month, irrespective of how many children you have. You do not pay IT or NICs on the part of the salary you take in vouchers or 'sacrifice'.

The amount you save depends upon the level of tax and NI you pay, but it can be up to £1,195 a year, and levels may well rise in future.

Use your vouchers for example for:

- Registered child minders, nurseries and play schemes.
- Out-of-hours clubs on school premises run by a school or local authority.
- In England only, childcare given in the child's own home by an approved person (but not a relative).

- In Scotland only, childcare given in the child's own home by registered childcare agencies.

- Approved foster carers (the care must be for a child who is not the foster carer's foster child).

- HMRC have more details and if one is not offered, push your employer to set up a scheme for all employees.

TOP TIP

If both parents work for employers operating schemes, both can join even if there's only one child involved, doubling up the tax savings to £2,390 max!

Give to receive

Taxpayers can be doubly bountiful to favourite charities or good causes (including most universities, amateur sports clubs and museums) with the help of the taxman. Make a donation and the taxman treats this as coming from your 'after tax' income. He enhances the donation by the tax element and if you are a 40 percenter – a £78 gift becomes £100 in the hands of the charity and you can claim tax back of £18 through your self-assessment return. Give that to charity too and the taxman is really helping!

Perks from Santa

Every year, Christmas comes around and thoughts turn to business gifts but what exactly are the tax rules surrounding these? Employers can avoid getting caught for tax by getting up to speed.

Giving away free samples of your products is 100% deductible, and so are gifts carrying a conspicuous advertisement for the business, but only up to £50 per person. Gifts of food, drink, tobacco and vouchers receive no tax deduction, even if less than £50.

Tip 1. Give away those bottles of booze and claim back the VAT on the purchase price with a clear conscience, but you should add the expense back to your net profits before calculating the tax due.

Tip 2. The £50 limit applies to the total value of gifts made to one person in a year, meaning you could give a customer five £10 crystal glasses as long as they carry your name or logo.

Tip 3. Don't go to the expense of getting diaries specially printed or the glasses engraved. Get company stickers printed and apply them liberally, making sure you apply them to the gift and not just to the wrapping!

Blame and claim

Complaints are common into the conduct of HMRC. Do it properly and you may successfully claim back costs and compensation. The way to do it, if an initial phone call fails to rectify the position is:

- Contact the Complaints Manager in writing, including all facts, what went wrong, when, and who was involved. Keep a copy, and don't forget to include your reference numbers.

- They will respond, usually within 30 days. They have staff employed specifically for complaints – so you're not alone!

- Still unhappy – then the next steps are the Adjudicator or try your M.P. for free impartial advice.

- HMRC regularly apologise, explain and refund certain costs.

- Keep any receipts and you stand a good chance of being reimbursed for postage, phone calls and professional fees.

- They will also pay out for worry and distress arising from their mistakes or unreasonable delays. So don't give up – it may take time but it could be worth the trouble and make you feel better too.

Summary

With all claims, remember the taxman's mantra "no receipt, no claim" – it's as simple as that! And remember - if it's not written down it never happened!

> "Next to being shot at and missed, nothing is really quite as satisfying as an Income Tax refund.

F.J. Raymond

chapter 7
Tax return tips

More than 9 million self-assessment tax returns are issued annually. In 2006 over 870,000 people neglected to file on time and invariably the end of January sees a last minute dash to the finishing post – but don't rely on the post! If time is tight you could personally pop it through the letterbox of the local tax office – but beware, not all local tax centres have them.

Beat the clock by filing online—even at midnight—but you have to be registered and receive a user ID – too late by 31st January.

Penalties and interest may well work out at a large percentage of what you owe – and why throw it at the taxman, he's got enough of your hard earned dough already!

Get started online

File online, get your tax calculation and acknowledgement and get on with something more exciting.

1. Register and enrol at www.hmrc.gov.uk.

2. Select the "self assessment" link in "do it online" and follow the prompts.

3. Create your password and get a User ID to use when you login.

4. An Activation PIN will be sent to you by post within 7 working days.

Who needs a tax return?

You are a likely candidate for self-assessment if...

- You work for yourself – self-employed, or in partnership.
- You are a company director.
- You are a Name or Member of Lloyd's insurance.
- You are a Minister of Religion.
- You have income from letting property or land.
- You receive other untaxed income and the tax cannot be collected through PAYE.
- You receive income from a trust or settlement.
- You have taxable foreign income, or are a non-resident landlord.
- You have sold or given away chargeable assets exceeding certain annual limits, or want to claim a capital loss, or make a CGT claim or election.
- ...and there's more, so you may have to call HMRC to check.

What counts as 'taxable income'?

Taxable Income includes:

- Earnings from employment.
- Earnings from self-employment.
- Most pensions income (state, company and personal).
- Interest on savings.
- Share dividends.
- Rental income.
- Trust income.

Non-taxable income

There are certain sorts of income that you never pay tax on. These include certain benefits, special pensions and income from tax-exempt accounts, all ignored when working out your tax.

Don't hold your breath

As the tax office operates a "process now, check later" system, your return will be captured and processed by computer, which will churn out your acknowledgement and calculation.

This does not mean they have accepted your figures or agree they are correct. They have a further year following the deadline filing date in which to challenge your figures and make enquiries.

If you want to amend your own return you can do so up to a year after the regular 31st January filing date (or the date the form is received by HMRC), provided the Revenue have not got in first and raised an enquiry into it.

From 2007/08 onwards, for those filing online, the deadline remains 31st January. The pen and paper brigade have to get their skates on and file by 31st October as HMRC push to encourage online filing for all.

Keep in touch

Difficulty paying the bill? Don't delay, 'phone the taxman and offer an arrangement because he has to listen. Ignore him, however, and legal action will swiftly follow.

D-day – delivery day

- The well-publicised 30th September deadline was never in fact a deadline at all, and there were no penalties for failing to file by 30th September.

- From 2007/08, paper returns must be lodged by 31st October and HMRC will calculate your tax for you.

- Online returns have until 31st January and a calculation is generated.

- Submitting forms after this date, with any late payment of tax, results in a penalty along with interest on top.

- Unpaid tax also attracts two lots of 5% surcharges on the amount outstanding.

- If the return has still not been submitted after 6 months, there is a further £100 fixed penalty.

- File by 31st October and underpayments of tax can be clawed back through next year's PAYE code, giving you a distinct cash flow advantage.

- For new sources of income arising in a tax year, or amounts subject to CGT (Capital Gains Tax), notification has to be made to the Revenue by 5th October following the year of assessment. If a return has not been received and there is income to be declared, it's your job to request a return to avoid further penalties.

Top ten penalty hits

1. Automatic fixed penalty of £100 if tax return is filed late. The penalty is £100 per partner for partnership returns.

2. Further £100 penalty if the return is still outstanding six months later.

3. The penalty cannot exceed the tax liability for the year for individuals. No such restriction exists for a penalty charge on a partnership return.

4. Interest is levied at the 'prescribed rate' on tax paid late.

5. To force delivery HMRC can impose daily penalties of up to £60. A daily penalty is per partner for a partnership return.

6. Tax geared penalties are chargeable where failure to file continues for more than twelve months and again this cannot exceed tax liability for the year.

7. There is an automatic surcharge amounting to 5% of any balancing payment for the tax year which is unpaid after 28 days.

8. A further surcharge is levied at 5% of any tax still unpaid more than six months from the due date.

9. Interest is levied on surcharges unpaid after 30 days.

10. Simply being on the ball can save you a fortune and a veritable paper mountain.

Example tax timeline (2007-08)

6th April	—	Tax Returns issued for previous tax year.
31st May	—	Latest date to be given your P60.
5th July	—	Deadline to apply for tax credits from 5th April.
6th July	—	Last date to receive your P11D/P9D.
31st July	—	Second tax instalments due for previous tax year.
5th October	—	Deadline to notify HMRC of new income sources or capital gains for previous tax year.
31st October	—	Paper Tax Return filing date to ensure HMRC calculate your tax or code out underpayments.
31st January	—	Tax Return online filing deadline.
	—	First Interim tax payment due for current year.
	—	Balancing payment due for previous year.
5th April	—	End of tax year.

Summary

- Assemble all the information needed to complete the returns.

- Download duplicates from the Revenue's website.

- Keep a copy of tax return guidance notes – they are useful.

- Compare this year's return with the previous year's re significant changes.

- Do not include pence in the return, apart from payments on account.

- Don't include ISA and PEP income, but include state pension, dividend and bank interest.

- For properties sold (not main residences) ensure you get the completion statements and include original costs and any improvement expenditure.

- Where dividend warrants have been lost and receipts cannot be traced via the bank statements, use **www.ukdividends.com** or write to the company secretary of the company concerned.

- Sign and date it or it will bounce back.

- If calculating your own tax, note how much tax you owe and when to pay it as Revenue Statements can take ages to arrive.

> "The hardest thing
> in the world to
> understand is
> Income Tax.

Albert Einstein

chapter 8
Crack the code

HMRC deals with the affairs of over 36 million taxpayers and it is no surprise to see that year on year they make mistakes — well, nobody's perfect. However with around 60% of all their PAYE errors affecting the amount of tax payable and relating to tax codes, you may well be a victim.

The average underpayment of tax is about £250 and overpayments run at around £290. So if you are in the group classed as 'complicated', that is with pensions, agency income, benefits in kind or multiple jobs, watch out for coding errors and SHOUT!

The coding enigma

A tax code is usually made up of one letter and several numbers, for example: 119L or K486.

If your tax code is a number followed by a letter and you multiply the number in your tax code by 10, you'll get the total amount of income you can earn in a year before paying tax. The letter shows employers how the number should be adjusted following any changes to allowances announced by the Chancellor.

But if your tax code begins with K, the number indicates how much must be added to your taxable income.

Common tax code letters explained:-

L   –   used if you are eligible for the basic personal allowance.

P   –   used if you are aged 65 to 74 and eligible for the full personal allowance.

V   –   used if you are 65 to 74, eligible for the full personal allowance and the full married couple's allowance (for those born before 6 April 1935 and aged under 75) and estimated to be liable at the basic rate of tax.

Y   –   used if you are aged 75 or over and eligible for the full personal allowance.

T   –   used if there are any other items HMRC needs to review in your tax code, or if you ask HMRC not to use any of the other tax code letters listed above.

K   –   used when your total allowances are less than your total deductions.

All change

You must keep HMRC informed of any changes in your circumstances, for example if:

- You get married or separate and either of you was born before 6 April 1935.
- You start to receive a second income or pension.
- The amount of untaxed income you get increases or reduces.

If you do not do this you could end up paying the wrong amount of tax.

If HMRC changes your tax code, you should receive a 'notice of coding' from your Tax Office. Keep all notices of coding for reference in case you have any questions or need to check that you are paying the right level of tax.

Numberless codes

If your tax code has two letters but no number, or is the letter D followed by a zero, it normally indicates that you have two or more sources of income and that all of your allowances have been applied to your main job.

BR – used when all your income is taxed at the basic rate – most commonly used for a second job.

DO – used when all your income is taxed at the higher rate – again commonly for second jobs.

NT – used when no tax is to be taken from your income.

If you have two jobs, it's likely that all of your second income will be taxed at the basic or higher rate – depending on how much you earn. This is because all of your allowances will have been used against the income from your main job.

Be professional

The Revenue has a whole list of professional subscriptions, which qualify for tax relief and can be included in your code number. It's likely that yours will qualify so give them a call and make a claim not only for the current year but the previous six too.

Check it out

The best and potentially most profitable New Year resolution for anyone is "I will monitor my tax code".

All employees, and many pensioners, should have a tax code. It's the red light from the HMRC to employers of the tax allowances due to the employee. HMRC send you a code at least once a year and you really should check that it's correct.

All you need to do is review what's on your coding notice and query immediately anything you don't understand. Incorrect codes, and they often happen, mean that the wrong amount of tax is being deducted and it can take a few weeks and pay days to rectify.

Here are some common areas that give rise to coding errors:

- A continued charge for a benefit you no longer have is a regular occurrence (like a company car).

- Those over 65 should always check that they have been given their higher age allowances. HMRC don't always spot 65th or 75th birthdays and being 65 or 75 at any time during the tax year qualifies you for higher allowances.

- Alternatively you may have estimated 'tips' included that are too high.

- Check that any deduction from allowances in respect of a state pension or taxable state benefit is the correct annual amount.

Don't miss out

It is notoriously difficult to persuade the taxman to grant you work-related expenses. Below are a selection of the flat rate expenses you can claim as agreed by your trade union or organisation to cover tools and special clothing. You can claim them back for the previous six years too, to give you a nice windfall!

Industry	Occupation	Deduction (2004/05 onwards)
Agriculture	All workers	70
Fire Service	Uniformed officers	60
Healthcare	Ambulance staff	110
Heating	Pipefitters & Plumbers	100
Police	Uniformed officers	55
Shipyards	Many tradesmen	115
Textiles	Carders	85
Non-wood	Artificial Limb Makers	90

There are many more categories and literally something for nearly everyone – but not for Tax Inspectors or Accountants!

Quick tip

HAVING A DOMESTIC

Employ domestic staff and you will have to deduct IT and NIC from your nanny or chauffeur's wages. Help is out there. A simplified PAYE scheme exists, subject to earnings limits, to ease the admin burden.

"A fine is a tax for doing something wrong. A tax is a fine for doing something right.

Anon

chapter 9
Starting in business

Money is cited as a key reason why people shy away from starting a venture of their own – and fear of a complex tax system can be a real barrier to a budding entrepreneur. You don't need to face the demons on *Dragon's Den* – help is at hand from a variety of sources:

- Young Enterprise.
- Business Link.
- The Prince's Trust (for 16-30 year olds).
- Small Business Service.
- New Entrepreneur Scholarships (in some areas).
- HMRC.

Start as you mean to go on

Develop good habits and a routine from day one:

- Set aside half an hour a week for record keeping.
- Record all expenditure.
- Keep bills and receipts.
- Use Excel or basic accounting software to list all income and expenses.

And consider the following areas for your claims:

- Capital Expenditure, i.e. office equipment, vehicles.
- Stock.
- Motor and Travel Expenses.
- Telephone.
- Printing Stationery and Postage.
- Marketing and Advertising.
- Bank and Finance Charges.
- Legal and Professional Fees.
- Percentage of household bills for working at home.

Employed v self-employed status

Unfortunately it is not sufficient for a person to merely decide that he or she is self-employed and turn up for work as such. OK, for many it will be clear exactly what their status is.

The owner of the corner shop selling your morning paper is not likely to be an employee, but conversely the waitress serving you your dinner is, almost without doubt, one. But between these extremes there exists many less clearly defined engagements and these grey areas provide the taxman with rich pickings from an unsuspecting and largely tax ignorant workforce.

A person's tax and NICs directly flow from their employment status. An employee is a person who works under a "contract of service", whilst a person who works under a "contract for services" is self-employed and for the latter there can be distinct monetary and practical advantages.

IT and NIC legislation does not define 'contract of service' and it is up to both sides, HMRC and employers, to seek guidance from the employment status case law handed down by the Courts over the years. The Courts have identified factors that help to determine whether a particular contract amounts to employment or self-employment. Contracts do not have to be in writing, they can be written, oral, implied or a combination of all three. One thing for sure is, an extensive knowledge of these factors is required, as all carry different weight in the arguments.

HMRC consider the following relevant factors in determining status:

- Whether there is an ultimate right of control on the part of the engager over what tasks have to be done and where, when and how the services have to be performed.
- Whether personal service is required.
- Whether the worker has the right to provide a substitute or engage helpers.
- Who has to provide the equipment and materials?
- Whether the worker has a real risk of financial loss.
- Whether the worker has the opportunity to profit from sound management for example, by reducing overheads and organising work effectively.
- The basis of payment.
- Whether there are 'employee type' benefits like, sick pay, pensions, holiday pay.
- Whether the worker works exclusively for the engager.

- Whether the worker is 'part and parcel' of the engager's business.
- Whether there is a right of dismissal by notice period of specific length.
- Factors personal to the worker, i.e. number of engagements and business organisation.
- The intention of both parties from day one re. the employment status.

The correct procedure is to stand back and look at the big picture, to see whether, overall, a person is in business on his own account or is working as an employee in somebody else's business.

Unfortunately, should HMRC give an opinion which reclassifies someone as an 'employee' (particularly when they may have been working long-term on a self-employed basis) the additional tax and Class 1 NICs is due from the 'employer' plus charges to interest and penalties. A strong fight is needed, leaving no stone unturned in the fact-finding mission, and you may need to call in an expert.

New regulations have been introduced to deal with the practicalities of collecting tax when a worker is technically reclassified from "self employed" to "employed" and the employer has failed to make the proper deductions under PAYE (but where the worker has already paid his tax as a self-employed person under Self Assessment). This is essentially to make sure that the Revenue doesn't get the tax twice!

What's your line?

1. **Sole trader**
   This means that you're an individual who is self-employed. You will pay Income Tax through the Self Assessment system, as well as Class 2 and Class 4 National Insurance and VAT if you reach the registration threshold.

2. **Partnership**
   If there are two or more people in your business, you might want to consider a formal deed of partnership. A solicitor will help you with this.

3. **Limited company**
   You can use a company registration agent to buy a company 'off the shelf' or you can create your own and register it at Companies House.

4. **Company director**
   You are also an employee of the company, so there are different National Insurance and PAYE obligations.

5. **Contractor under the Construction Industry Scheme (CIS)**
   You run a business and engage subcontractors for construction.

6. **Contractor**
   You are paid by a contractor to do construction industry work.

Simple weekly record sheets

For the new small business the sheet below may help you keep a track of daily income and expenses and keep your accountant happy:

BUSINESS NAME					
WEEK ENDED					
RECEIPTS					
DAY	DATE	CASH		CHEQUES	CREDIT CARDS

Daunted? Don't be! To be certain that you're on the right track from day one why not take advantage of the many free workshops provided by HMRC's Advisory Teams. They offer non-judgemental advice to boost confidence and encourage new business starters and cover record keeping, payroll and much more.

PAYMENTS

DATE	PAYEE	CASH		CHEQUE	
	TOTAL				
CONTROL					
	Balance B/forward				
	Takings				
	Drawn from Bank				
	Payments				
	Banked				
	Carried Forward				

NIC, NIC!

Almost everyone who works for a living pays National Insurance. It goes towards pensions, benefits and healthcare.

1. **Class 1 NICs** – payable by anyone who is employed.

2. **Class 2 NICs** – payable by the self-employed.

3. **Class 3 NICs** – voluntary, to cover shortfalls in your NI contributions and protect your entitlement to State Pension and bereavement benefits.

4. **Class 4 NICs** – payable by most self-employed people. They are merely another form of tax, being a percentage of your annual taxable profits.

Small business – big ideas

The government is always proud to publicise what they have done for small businesses, unfortunately most used to be big businesses! Scan this checklist to help you keep ahead of the game.

1. If your business is a Limited Company it often makes sense to get your money out by a combination of salary, benefits in kind, and dividends. Take advice. Recent changes in the law can reveal advantages but also pitfalls.

2. If you are paying your spouse a salary it must be at a commercial rate for the job, they must actually work and be paid personally.

3. Pension contributions are tax deductible – effectively costing maybe only 60p for each £1 invested. Go for it, if you don't provide for your retirement, no-one else will!

4. If you are a sole trader consider taking your spouse into partnership – but again take advice.

5. Investing in a new car, computer or other business assets? Get tax relief a lot quicker by making the investment shortly before, rather than shortly after, your year-end.

6. If your business has made losses make sure that they are being used to reduce your current tax bills as far as possible.

7. If you run a one-man-band limited company beware of the IR35 rules. Odds on you will have heard of them – your accountant certainly has!

8. Tell the Taxman of any changes to your company cars as soon as they happen.

9. Make the most of tax-free benefits in kind for your staff, e.g:
   - Provide mobile phones.
   - Give luncheon vouchers.
   - Subsidise certain transport to and from work.
   - Provide workplace nurseries and crèches.
   - Pay relocation expenses.
   - Spend up to £150 per person for the staff party.
   - Make cash awards for staff suggestion schemes.
   - Allow staff pool cars for business purposes.

10. Pay staff £5 a night for incidentals if they are away overnight on business (£10 if abroad).

11. Christmas gifts (normally a turkey, wine or chocolates) of around £25 per head are tax free.

12. Watch the use of those contractors and freelancers – the taxman often regards them as employees and will look to you for their tax.

13. A long service gift for those with more than 20 years service is tax-free—worth up to £50 for each year of service—that's £1,000 tax free for you both.

14. Employees working from home can have £2pw tax-free without providing any evidence that they have spent the money.

15. Keep on the top-side of the National Minimum Wage as HMRC are there to police the system.

16. Reduce your paperwork, ask HMRC for a dispensation for all tax neutral benefits and expenses. It will cut the hassle of P11Ds.

17. If you are going to employ people then it helps to get everything sorted out well in advance. Get the new employer's starter pack and CD Rom – it's all free. HMRC also provide free training for new employers and will even come out and help you – without judging you.

Time limits

Time is tight to notify HMRC that you have started in business – register with them for tax and NIC within 3 months of starting, by completing the form CWF1 – or face a £100 penalty charge.

It's my money

If you are self-employed the wages you take for yourself are called "Drawings". Record everything you take at the time, as the taxman casts a keen eye on this area of your business. If your drawings seem to him to be on the low side (compared to say the national average wage) you'll be a prime target for an investigation. The way you live is very interesting to them as is how you afford it, and it's a red rag to a bull to most taxpayers.

Don't be surprised when they compare your drawings to:

1. Your property and cars.

2. Lifestyle indicators (holidays, schools etc).

3. National levels.

4. Year on year fluctuations.

5. Wages you pay to others.

Self-preservation

A set of complete and accurate financial records is the best protection from a tax investigation – they are the bedrock of your accounts and tax return. Unless they can find holes in your records Inspectors cannot justify looking further into your private affairs.

GOOD RECORDING WILL SAVE YOU MONEY!

Record round up

An investigating officer is entitled to look at them but:

- Offer access to them at your accountant's office rather than hand them over at his, and stay in control.

- There is nothing in law to enforce their delivery direct to his door.

- He's allowed 'reasonable access' only, so offer them for a day – otherwise he'll hang on to them for months and who knows what he'll do with them.

- He uses computer data interrogation software, so initially offer hard copy printouts of your computerised books to cut down the questions he may raise.

- If he does take them away – don't forget about them and ask for them back quickly, they are yours.

- He has the right to take copies. Reduce the number by doing them for him if he flags up the ones he wants – it will give you a big clue as to what he's looking for.

Finding a link

Keep business and private cash separate. Open a separate business account. Bank all cash and cheques in there and pay all business bills by cheque. Easier said than done for some, but to avoid Revenue scrutiny do not link your private accounts by using them for business deposits or withdrawals. If you do, HMRC can have access to these as part of the business records and this can open a can of worms and drag out an enquiry unnecessarily.

TOP TIP

Arrange for your drawings to be transferred into a private account each week or month by standing order.

Big CIS

If you work in the construction industry in the UK, your records will be ruled by the new scheme, which came into effect from April 2007. Stringent rules apply to the recording of payments and deductions of tax, with onerous form filling requirements. Follow them religiously and your bible will be HMRC Booklet CIS340 – a great basic guide.

Keeping it in the family

If wages are paid to your spouse (or children) avoid HMRC challenge by:

1. Making sure recognised duties are carried out.

2. The wage is a commercially acceptable level per hour.

3. The money is actually paid to them.

Generally, housekeeping money paid to a wife (with few actual duties) into the joint bank account can be difficult to justify as a valid claim in your accounts.

Don't ask – don't get

Inspectors notoriously work under this concept and a vast number of taxpayers automatically respond by handing over wholesale whatever he asks for, regardless of his right to them in law. So keep your 'private' bank statements, savings accounts, credit card statements and diaries that way, when they have no relevance in checking the accuracy of your return. Working on the belief that the self-employed rarely return the full extent of their profits, the Revenue are desperate to home in on your personal financial records, so unless they have good reason, keep them to yourself.

Own consumption

If you are in a retail trade it may be quite normal to take items out of stock for your family's own use. Did you know that you should pay for, or account for, everything taken at its retail price, not at cost? Put everything through the books at full price – or the taxman will be looking for the extra from you.

Take the long view

Stand back and ask yourself "In the eyes of an outsider can I manage to live on this income?" Doubtful? Well use the tax return spaces to tell HMRC if you have other money available— spouse's income, legacies, gifts, bank borrowing—or at least discuss it with your accountant. Try preparing a simple record of your outgoings for a month, in case you are challenged at a later date.

Jacks of all trades

A methodology used for selecting prime cases for investigation, is to compare your gross profit with other similar types of trades, sometimes within similar postcode areas. Fall below their 'norm' and you are in the frame. It goes without saying that cash-based businesses go straight into their high risk 'pool'. That, combined with a low gross profit rate and low drawings, will leave you reaching for the life belt.

Going for the little man

Nearly half of sole trader investigations are into those declaring an annual turnover of under £50,000, or £1,000 per week, largely those in the risky cash handling area, having home-made record keeping systems. The taxman is rubbing his hands in these cases as they are notoriously easy to railroad into a monetary settlement, with little resistance, within about 12 months. It's less simple for them in company enquiries with more robust records, which take longer but often yield more.

TOP TIP

For comparatively small cost, businesses can take out insurance to cover the professional fees involved in fighting the Revenue. I would recommend that you speak to your accountant about it to ensure the free back up of a specialist is firmly on your side.

Summary

Minimise the risk of a large tax settlement by being ready for the Inspector's challenge.

- Record all takings – including "ancillary" amounts from, say vending machines, scrap sales, commission, tips, etc.

- Record events adversely affecting your income – bad weather, power cuts, strike action, road works, illness, competitors.

- Note all stock given away to charity, and for raffle prizes, etc.

- Record all items taken for own use or in the case of a service industry, time spent working on your own home, etc.

- Record waste – from the fish and chips or perishables thrown away, to stock destroyed in a flood.

- Report incidences of theft by staff to the police and obtain a crime number or at least note your records as fully as possible.

- Shoplifting levels should be monitored and noted – it could be around 5% and will affect your gross profit rate.

- Track increases in overheads – heat and light, carriage and wrappings, etc.

- Reconcile cash every night, noting and investigating any discrepancies.

- Bank all takings regularly, drawing cash needed for wages etc. from the bank.

- Keep petty cash secure, obtain receipts for all items, and balance weekly.

Remember the taxman's 'foot in the door' is through your records – and he can go back up to 20 years if he thinks your records are less than robust.

"I believe we should all pay our tax bill with a smile. I tried but they wanted cash.

Anon

chapter 10
In the know

The inception of HMRC's Tax Evasion Hotline (see the website) has provided a cost effective income stream for them. It enables, nay encourages, Joe Public to anonymously grass up anyone they suspect of denying the crown its fair dues across the full range of taxes – with no detail too trivial for them. It gives a new meaning to 'the shopping channel'!

But even without your help the Taxman is constantly accessing intelligence and data on you all. It never ceases to amaze me how little people know about the inner workings of HMRC. Ignorance is bliss you may think – but of course it is never an acceptable excuse.

One of my lectures is devoted to exposing the vast level of information that HMRC can be sitting on unbeknown to you – and it's by far my most popular one, even if some of the audience leave visibly shaken!

As a department, HMRC talk incessantly about "closing the tax gap" and has a real economic need to bring in as much extra cash as possible. The only "gap" I continue to see is the gaping hole in their ability to understand how we, their "customers", struggle to run a business in the real world. These "behind the scenes" tactics help swell their coffers.

Forewarned is forearmed

Here's a list of some of the sources of their information...

- Auctioneers – who return sales of chattels.
- Estate Agents.
- Letting agents.
- Registers from pubs and clubs, of entertainers and discos.
- Registration of yachts and aircrafts.
- DVLA (registered keepers).
- Financial information on your annuities, mortgages.
- Registers of driving instructors.
- Bank and building society accounts including ISAs.
- Shipping registries.
- Casino membership lists.
- Companies house.
- Informers – anonymous or otherwise.
- Council tax/business rates.
- Housing benefit claimants and landlords.
- Offshore bank account holders.
- Overseas tax authorities.
- Certain surveillance.
- Snooping at cards/adverts in shop windows.
- Drive bys – identifying executive homes and signs of wealth, e.g. swimming pools, pricey car.
- Reviews of local papers for details of interest like planning approvals, articles about local businesses, car sales, etc.

That little hideaway

Apart from the air raid shelter at the bottom of the garden it's virtually impossible to hide a property from the Revenue. They have access to a vast amount of information on you such as:

- Stamp Duty is administrated by HMRC, so they have records from valuation offices on all properties bought and sold.

- Housing benefit details of rents paid to landlords.

- Council tax/business rate paid.

- Returns from estate agents or letting agents of rents collected.

- The voters lists – proving categorically to a vigilant taxman who lived where and when.

- The local papers, checking properties for sale, particularly "home of the week" where people just cannot help showing off their costly interiors and luxurious lifestyles.

- Information on properties purchased abroad, even noting information from the likes of TV's "A Place in the Sun", where prospective purchasers reveal their innermost financial secrets in order to acquire that luxury second home.

- Finally don't forget the Taxman, the Vatman, and their families all need a home – and it could be next door to yours!

EU confidantes

The UK and other EU member states, are legally obliged to exchange information with each other to combat international tax evasion and avoidance. Since 2005 this was bolstered by the EU Savings Directive requiring automatic reporting of savings income paid cross-border to residents of other member states. Agreements have been reached with non-EU members too.

Snouts!

Much unsolicited information comes HMRC's way from informers. Common examples are, as you would expect, spurned ex-spouses and employees and former business partners. With the much-publicised "Evaders Hotline" going strong, the prevalence is for businesses to attempt to wipe out the local competition by a call to the taxman, however spurious! If the information can be substantiated it's an odds-on favourite for investigation – well why wouldn't they? But you'll be kept in the dark, as Inspectors are instructed never to divulge the source of information. You'll hear that "there is information in the hands of the department" and it's up to you to put 2 and 2 together.

The letter of the law

Statute enables them to issue formal notices to anyone they think has:

A. Been in receipt of money belonging to others;

B. Paid out fees, commission or other monies not subject to PAYE.

You have no choice but to comply!

Summary

Over the years the volume and quality of information coming HMRC's way has improved, sadly the same cannot be said of their staff! With cutbacks and reorganisation, morale can be low. However those who stay the course are increasingly trained to take a much more aggressive approach. The above should help cut the risk of a nasty surprise. Don't have sleepless nights!

My final message to you…

For most people, coming face to face with a tax inspector in a small room will never happen, but should you be one of the chosen few, I hope that these tips will provide you with a degree of "know how" or at least you will "know who" to approach for help – me!

Paying less tax and suffering fewer sleepless nights is what we all crave and I hope I have offered some painless and lighter-hearted methods for beating the system, which is becoming more and more powerful under the merged forces of HM Revenue and Customs.

You are up against a tax system that is neither fair nor logical and just when you thought you'd grasped it, they move the goal posts each year with a new Finance Act, which can turn an established practice on its head and close that lucrative loophole. It's what makes my job so very satisfying, along with my lovely clients who deserve the best possible defence.

Good luck!

Abbreviations

Basic Rate of Tax	**BR**
Capital Gains Tax	**CGT**
Civil Investigation of Fraud	**CIF**
Code of Practice	**COP**
Child Tax Credit	**CTC**
Child Tax Fund	**CTF**
Civil Partnersip	**CP**
Construction Industry Scheme	**CIS**
Corporation Tax	**CT**
Department for Work and Pensions	**DWP**
HM Revenue and Customs	**HMRC**
Income Tax	**IT**
Inheritance Tax	**IHT**
National Insurance	**NI**
National Insurance Contributions	**NICs**
Pay As You Earn	**PAYE**
Resident and Ordinarily resident	**R/OR**
Valuation Office Agency	**VOA**
Value Added Tax	**VAT**
Working Tax Credit	**WTC**

Useful websites

Lindsay Henson, tax expert, presenter and author of this book
www.lindsayhenson.co.uk

Networking group for women in business or the professions
www.workwisewomen.co.uk

Guy Bolam, financial adviser, practical, holistic and never boring
www.bolamrose.com

Office of the Public Guardian
www.guardianship.gov.uk

Secretarial services, PA, PR and GF (Girl Friday)
www.flmsecretarialservices.co.uk

HMRC home page
www.hmrc.gov.uk

If it all goes wrong
www.adjudicatorsoffice.gov.uk

Starting up in business
www.businesslink.gov.uk

Pensions and benefits
www.dwp.gov.uk

Identity fraud
www.identity-theft.org.uk

Council tax/rates queries
www.voa.gov.uk

Index

What's on the Taxman's ipod?

THE HIT PARADE

1. *The Taxman* by the Beatles

2. *Lazing on a Sunny Afternoon* by The Kinks
   (with the line *The Taxman's taken all my dough*!)

3. *You Can't Always Get What You Want*
   by The Rolling Stones

4. *Taxman, Thief* by Cheap Trick

5. *Money, Money, Money* by Abba

6. *Money for Nothing* by Dire Straits

7. *Black Money* by Culture Club

8. *Money (That's What I Want)* by The Beatles

9. *Give Me Some Truth* by Travis

10. *It's Yer Money I'm After Baby* by Wonder Stuff

11. *Stand and Deliver* by Adam Ant

12. *Everyday I Think of Money* by The Stereophonics

13. *Rain, Tax (It's Inevitable)* by Celine Dion

14. *Take the Money and Run* by Steve Miller

15. *Billy No Mates* by Liane Carroll.

'The Greatest Tips in the World' books

Sex Tips
ISBN 978-1-905151-74-5

Travel Tips
ISBN 978-1-905151-73-8

Slimming & Healthy Living Tips
ISBN 978-1-905151-31-8

Wedding Tips
ISBN 978-1-905151-27-1

Tax Tips
ISBN 978-1-905151-43-1

Pet Recipe books

The Greatest Feline Feasts in the World
ISBN 978-1-905151-50-9

The Greatest Doggie Dinners in the World
ISBN 978-1-905151-51-6

'The Greatest in the World' DVDs

The Greatest in the World – Gardening Tips

The Greatest in the World – Yoga Tips

The Greatest in the World – Cat & Kitten Tips

The Greatest in the World – Dog & Puppy Tips

For more information about currently available
and forthcoming book and DVD titles please visit:

www.thegreatestintheworld.com

or write to:

The Greatest in the World Ltd
PO Box 3182
Stratford-upon-Avon
Warwickshire CV37 7XW
United Kingdom

Tel / Fax: +44(0)1789 299616
Email: info@thegreatestintheworld.com

The author

Working as an Inland Revenue Tax Inspector in 1992, Lindsay took the somewhat risky decision to turn her back upon the cosy job for life with indexed linked pension, and moved out of her comfort zone to become the proverbial "gamekeeper turned poacher".

On the basis that everyone deserves a defence and armed with invaluable inside knowledge, she signed up with a national firm of chartered accountants to offer her services in representing those who fall foul of the Taxman.

Using her experience from the other side she has developed her hands-on approach to keep the taxman's hands off your money. Life is never dull and invariably there's a humorous side – often at the Revenue's expense.

Lindsay is approachable and fair, and always goes that extra mile. She guest lectures on cruise ships, as well as speaking to fellow professionals. "Talking Tax" is what Lindsay does.

Visit **www.lindsayhenson.co.uk**